MOVING
FROM THE
MARGINS

MOVING
FROM THE
MARGINS

a Chicana voice on public policy

ADELA
DE LA
TORRE

THE UNIVERSITY OF ARIZONA PRESS
TUCSON

The University of Arizona Press
© 2002 The Arizona Board of Regents
All rights reserved
♾ This book is printed on acid-free, archival-quality paper.
Manufactured in the United States of America
First printing

07 06 05 04 03 02   6 5 4 3 2 1

Library of Congress Cataloging-in-Publication Data
Torre, Adela de la.
Moving from the margins: a Chicana voice on public policy /
Adela de la Torre
p. cm.
"Most articles that appear in this book were first published as commentaries
that Adela de la Torre wrote for the *Los Angeles Times* between 1992 and
1998."
Includes bibliographical references and index.
ISBN 0-8165-1990-0 (cloth: alk. paper) — ISBN 0-8165-1991-9
(pbk.: alk. paper)
1. Mexican Americans—California—Politics and government. 2. Mexican
Americans—California—Social conditions. 3. California—Politics and
government—1951– 4. Political planning—California. 5. California—Social
conditions. 6. California—Ethnic relations. 7. Torre, Adela de la—Political
and social views. I. Title.
F870.M5 T67 2002
320'.6'09794—dc21

2001004399

British Library Cataloguing-in-Publication Data
A catalogue record for this book is available from the British Library.

Para mis hijas, Gaby y Adelita, y para mis sobrinos, Esteban, Nic, Samuel, Vesa, Marisa, y Miguel, que siempre mantengan sus valores y sus sueños. Para mi mamá, Herminia, por su apoyo, y para mi abuela Adela, quien me dió mis raices y mi idioma.

CONTENTS

PREFACE

When I was a child growing up in northern California, my world was full of the sounds and voices of migrants from other lands. The brisk brogue of "Auntie Ruth" and the dust bowl drawl of Aunt Mary encircled my youth with a tapestry of syncopated sounds that complemented my own Mexican cultural heritage. Much of what I know and who I am reflects an experience cultivated by these accented voices with their opinions on how daily life should move forward. From this extended family of neighbors and friends, I saw a world that was different from that of many of my peers, yet it prepared me for my lifelong inquiry into the symmetry and differences between ethnic groups.

My grandmother, Adela, a Mexican immigrant who had married a young widower shortly after Mexico's civil war, had migrated through the Texas panhandle to settle and raise her three children in the heart of California's San Joaquin Valley. It was here she would lose a husband, raise a family, and soon migrate to follow her eldest daughter, Matiana, as she entered one of the great public universities of the world, the University of California (UC) at Berkeley. Her youngest daughter, my mother, Hermina, followed her big sister's path, earning a degree from Berkeley in 1948. Uncle Paco, returning from World War II, settled in nearby Oakland to work and occasionally visit on weekends with our growing family. Between two unsuccessful marriages and struggles with *la botella* (the bottle), my *Tío* (Uncle) Paco would surface on weekends as my loving godfather who slipped *café con azucar* (coffee with sugar) in my *leche caliente* (hot milk) as my grandmother flipped flour tortillas on the heated *comal* (griddle) of our kitchen stove. From a child's vantage point, I saw life as an endless array of visitors and family members who would share food, laughter and *cuentos* (stories) around our kitchen table. Life was always about sharing experiences and opening doors for others. Laughter, not wealth, was the gauge for a successful day—ending in the soft bed I shared with my *abuelita* (grandmother), who enveloped me with her warmth and compassion.

Adventures in our daily life seemed limitless during that postwar era of the 1950s. How well we could navigate the East Bay cities with a bus token and a few *dulces* (candies). Any crises that we encountered could be overcome through prayer, and the "Dulce Madre," the Virgin Mary (or "Sweet Mother"). She would always watch over us as long as we honored her with our novenas and devotion. So much that I knew and expected as a child was rooted in a deep faith, a faith that was marked by such simplicity of rules, yet which provided us with unwavering hope for the future. This faith, combined with my grandmother's determination, overcame any sorrow in our lives.

And, yes, there was sorrow. Life was not easy for the youngest of Adela's daughters. Successful in her educational pursuits, but not in marriage, my mother struggled to raise her two daughters in a world where divorce was whispered of, but never acknowledged. As a single parent, she struggled to keep us financially afloat, as my grandmother assumed her role as matriarch once again. My mother's dreams of medical school were never realized, as she spent the next forty years teaching in a public classroom. Excelling in her new profession, she accepted her fate with a deep commitment and resolved that her daughters' choices would be different. Certainly, marriage would not seal their destinies.

Being surrounded by Latina women creating their own images of success affected the way I perceived the world. At an early age I was pushed to reach beyond my place as *la concentida* (the favorite) grandchild and namesake of my grandmother, Adela. Failure was not in my grandmother's vocabulary, nor was there shame in speaking her mother tongue. For her, as well as for my mother, hopes for us were tied to our educational success. One of my most vivid memories is of my grandmother taking me as a small child to the gates of the University of California, and telling me in Spanish, *Aquí vas a estudiar,* here is where you will study. Little did I know that twenty years later I would be completing my doctorate at UC, in a field in which few Mexican Americans have garnered success.

These images of my past shape my views. They shape both my sense of self and my love of a community where difference has its beauty and success may only be savored through struggle. Thus, the following collection of commentaries reflects how my sense of self informs my interpretation of political events that affect Mexican people. From this point of view, I use my more formal training in political economy to analyze current events and issues. It is clear from some of my writing that the personal is hardly removed from the political. At the same time, beyond the righteous indignation or poignant realism is a real attempt to look at the evidence in understanding how Latinas and Latinos are ignored or overlooked by our public commentators and how our views may be substantively different than those of others.

My goal in writing for the popular press was to offer a competing perspective on Latino issues in the mainstream media. Although journalism was not my formal vocation, I recognized early on that Latinas and Latinos need to take the risk of adding our (often dissenting) voices to the public debates affecting our communities. The majority of newspaper readers do not welcome a dissenting voice, particularly that of an educated Chicana. This certainly was true in the last decade of the twentieth century and still is today. Although significant gains have been made in California since the 1990s, a great many Latinos are still living on the margins of our society. Moving from those outer boundaries of poverty, discrimination, and neglect will require Latino representation at all levels of government, as well as in education (especially higher education), the medical professions, the media, and other industries. Equitable representation means being heard, and being heard is central to the success of Latinos in this decade and beyond. Without significant gains in these areas, and as long as millions of Latinos remain on the fringes of American political and economic life, voices that challenge the status quo will need to be raised.

ACKNOWLEDGMENTS

This book would not have been possible without the help and support of several people, and I am grateful for their assistance and participation in this project. First, I would like to thank my graduate students at the University of Arizona who assisted me at various stages of the book through their excellent research skills. They include Arlie Eicher, Erynn Masi de Casanova and Maritza De La Trinidad. In particular, Erynn was critical in completing the content analysis of the letters from the readers and Maritza had wonderful insights, analytical comments and constant optimism about this project. I would also like to extend my thanks to Mary Heffron Arno, articles editor of the Op Ed page of the *Los Angeles Times,* who provided me the opportunity to write for the *Times* and enhanced my commentaries with her excellent editorial skills, and Tom Gelsinon, from the Mexican American Studies & Research Center, who was also invaluable for his editorial expertise in reviewing this book. Finally, I would like to thank Patti Hartmann for supporting this project and the voices of Chicana/Latina scholars in her role as acquiring editor at the University of Arizona Press.

INTRODUCTION

As a writer of commentary and an economist, I felt it was important not to reduce my work to identity politics or an exotic viewpoint, but to speak to issues that molded California politics, and which created both ethnic consensus and cleavage. Over the five years that I wrote commentary for the *Los Angeles Times,* I learned not only from writing the articles, but also from the many letters, phone calls, and e-mail messages I received that challenged or championed my point of view. It is from these letters and messages that I recognized the enormous need to create a new dialogue of ideas, one that makes explicit our fears of integrating those who seem so different from us.

Most of my commentary pieces focus on issues that directly affect the Latina/o community. Issues such as immigration policy, education and child welfare are topics that create an immediate buzz of discussion in any urban household in the Southwest. They are at the heart of urban public policy in the twenty-first century. How are we going to control access to public services and ensure equal treatment to all legal residents? Should we continue bilingual education or should we look at other models for immigrant integration? What welfare policies provide the best incentives for families and young people? Is there a way to reconcile individual moral values with democratic moral ideals? Is a "color-blind" policy attainable in our lifetime or will racism require a vigilant proactive policy stance?

Many of these questions underscore the policy issues that I considered when writing on issues that affected the Latina/o community. Ultimately, as an integrationist, I felt compelled to address these issues as a reflection of my own middle-ground perspective. My goal was to cajole readers and voters to think beyond their own frames of reference to include a different point of view when weighing a decision that would affect millions of individual lives. Whether I was effective or not remains to be seen. However, as a writer, I hope that my words will have some influence on a reader's thoughts.

In the final analysis, this collection of columns from the *Los Angeles Times* and other selected commentary pieces explores what issues influenced recent ethnic politics in a state where division appears more common than unity. Moreover, my intent was to provide a glimpse of how Mexican Americans, California's largest ethnic minority, view issues differently than mainstream voters, and at the same time, how much they have in common with the current majority of California's electorate.

Mexican Americans rekindle the dreams of past immigrants, with their aspirations of a future for themselves and their children. Many conservative values concerning family and self-reliance are clearly present in how Mexican Americans view welfare reform and women's roles. At the same time, for a group that has experienced sustained exclusion in the political and economic realm, these traditional values are tempered by ethnically targeted reform measures (such as Propositions 209 and 227 in California) that seem to condone past exclusion and denigrate Mexican individuals and culture. Thus, attacks on bilingual education and immigrant rights develop a symbolism often ignored by those in the white mainstream media and in elected office.

Finally, the voice of racial discontent in a state like California is largely heard in the voice of the voting majority. Although it is a voice that Latinos may want to ignore, it is this dominant voice that has catapulted racial politics to the fore in California during the last ten years. No doubt this will continue unless we begin to listen to the growing voice of the new Latino electorate. By providing a forum for these competing voices in the same space, a new dialogue may emerge.

Fundamentally, we no longer are a common America. And there is no urgency within the electorate to create one vision. For example, witness the overwhelming electoral support of initiatives like California's Proposition 187, targeting illegal Latino immigrants; the anti–affirmative action initiative, Proposition 209; and Propositions 227 and 209 (Arizona), which challenge mandatory bilingual education. Beyond the polemics of who deserves publicly subsidized entitlements, and the issue of "reverse discrimination," is the end of white America's commitment to accelerating the economic and political assimilation of those unlike themselves. This is even more alarming given the recent U.S. census data that shows that Latinos have increased by 60 percent since the 1990 census, thus making Latinos one in eight of all Americans. Given these demographic figures, we no longer can support public policies that scapegoat and risk the integration of America's soon-to-be-largest minority group.

White America's obvious indifference goes beyond a future of continued balkanization across racial and ethnic groups. It may foreshadow an age when all Americans become prisoners of their race and ethnicity, with fewer prospects of straddling multiple boundaries of identity and group alliances. Such an America has little hope of success in this millennium if these lines continue to harden over time. With this in mind, we must argue not on moral imperatives, but rather on political and economic grounds that we must accelerate our dialogue on race and ethnicity, first to create a respectful understanding of our differences and then to negotiate a solution for targeted economic policies that accelerate the prospects for political assimilation of all groups. With such a dual strategy, we may then begin not only to give voice to our disagreements, but also to create tangent strategies for reform.

In many respects, the salience of this book is its attempt to give voice to group difference in interpreting public policy. During the years I wrote for the *Los Angeles Times,* I attempted to shift the context of public policy debates within the boundaries of the experience of the Mexican American community. At the same time, I was fortunate to elicit a considerable response on my perspectives from other voices within and outside this community. Sometimes the competing voices in these debates clearly illustrated the scars that define our political differences, yet at other times they suggested new bridges for an unusual dialogue between writer and reader.

In an attempt to provide a glimpse of this potential dialogue,

I have included, along with my own commentaries, selected reader responses—competing and concurring voices in this discussion. By including these responses, my goal is to give readers a sense of our divisions, but also the beginning points for a new dialogue.

MOVING
FROM THE
MARGINS

CHAPTER 1

IMMIGRATION

It's Immigration, All Over Again
When the economy is bad, politicians often look for scapegoats. Now, as in the 1970s, they've found immigration.

A few years back we by law legalized millions who had come illegally. It would seem all wrote their relatives to come and get in on life here. Legal Latinos and citizens of Latino heritage should resent the illegals right along with our voting majority.

—John Andrews

I don't apologize for the fact that it infuriates me when I hear third generation Americans that do not speak English . . . I believe that we are still encouraging racism with are appellations: African American, Mexican American, Korean American and the list goes on. We are Americans of a certain descent first and foremost.

—William Ash

IMMIGRATION REFORM and welfare reform have become the rallying cries of politicians of all persuasions in their battles to bolster their lagging popularity in the polls. Unfortunately, although estimating the costs and benefits of immigration should be honestly discussed, an emotional furor has overtaken the debate and made rational discussion on immigration impossible.

All of us who live in southern California see dark-skinned people who speak a foreign language in our schools, hospitals and churches. Aren't they undocumented, and shouldn't we trust our own judgment on this issue? Aren't we lucky that many of our elected officials confirm our suspicions for a change, or should we recognize that political survival requires the instinct to exploit others' insecurities for political advantage?

The ship of political fools who have embraced one another with new strategies to control the border include characters as diverse as Ross Perot, Pete Wilson, Bill Clinton and Dianne Feinstein. Their political motivation is transparent. Yet if we are to learn anything from history, it is that political duplicity often comes during times of economic strife. These strange bedfellows speak to the value of scapegoating a relatively powerless group, a much easier task than confronting the failure of Democrats and Republicans to address the severe problems of the California economy. As tiresome as the immigration debate has become, the new immigration debate is hardly different from the old. In particular, the striking similarities between the current policy deliberations and the discussions during the Carter Administration merit further reflection.

During the first year of his presidency, sensing frustration due to lagging productivity and inflation, Jimmy Carter sought to radically transform immigration law. The Carter plan included civil penalties for knowingly hiring undocumented workers, increased funding to control the border and an aid package to stimulate domestic employment in Mexico and control population growth. Although Carter's proposal was never supported by Congress, key elements of the plan were picked up by Sen. Alan K. Simpson (R-Wyo.) and Rep. Peter W. Rodino, Jr. (D-N.J.) in the Immigration Reform and Control Act (IRCA) of 1986. This law included Carter's amnesty provisions as well as civil penalties for knowingly hiring undocumented workers. For more than twenty years, this latter point has been acknowledged as the linchpin in controlling undocumented immigration to the United States. Other key provisions of IRCA were an alien-verification provision to access public services, federal funds for states disproportionately affected by the amnesty applicants, and guest-worker programs for seasonal agricultural employment.

Although IRCA was viewed as a failure by some academics, to a large extent the limitations of the 1986 law were due to lack of adequate enforcement and funding. Lax enforcement of employer sanctions was particularly true during the latter part of the Reagan Administration and the Bush Administration. As in the past, there was no need to heat up political discussions on immigration when the economy was on track. That much of the current discussion has been wasted on pitting one group against another and fueling ethnic mistrust is unfortunate. Media hysteria aside, enforcement of existing laws should be the first step in the reform process. It requires recognizing that the federal government must adequately fund enforcement, particularly in employment. New laws that strip away basic rights of citizenship would result in decades of litigation and squandered resources. The only solution to immigration reform is an economic policy that stimulates employment and economic growth, both here and in Mexico.

Los Angeles Times, September 15, 1993

Underneath California's Economy
Immigration policy needs to catch up with the marketplace, or both labor and the economy will continue to suffer.

The argument concerning undocumented workers should focus on the fact that there are so many skilled entry level jobs available in the service and agricultural sectors of the United States economy while many Latin American countries are unable to create enough jobs for their increasing populations. I propose a system to register workers willing to work in the posi-

tions that are readily available in the service and agricultural sectors here in the U.S.

—Eduardo Martinez

THE RECENT FANFARE over the "illegal" hiring practices of attorney general candidates Zoe Baird and Kimba Wood strikes a sore point for American workers concerned with maintaining jobs and working conditions. Long after the talk-show hosts exhaust their audiences with xenophobes who blame "illegals" for the failure of the American economy and deterioration of "American culture," the issue of the underground economy—the cash transaction economy that both legal and undocumented workers participate in—will remain. On Thursday in Sacramento, Assemblyman Richard Polanco (D-Los Angeles) will open hearings on "Immigrants, Immigration and the California Economy," in which legislators will address the impact of this underground economy.

The market for domestic services and child care is but a small segment of a labor market so interwoven into the fabric of southern California that its tapestry blankets the masses. Despite the economic significance of these workers, during recessionary times the workers become the lightning rod for public discourse about the inequities of our market system. But markets, including labor markets, do not respond to frustrated malcontents. Rather, they respond to incentives that induce transactions to occur. In a global economy in which wage differentials are so great, people will immigrate. Immigration from Mexico to the United States, or from Romania to Poland or the Philippines to Canada is inevitable.

Unfortunately, immigration law has not caught up with this dynamic flow. Unlike the glamorous North American Free Trade Agreement (NAFTA) that attempts to enhance the competitiveness of Canadian, Mexican and U.S. firms in global markets, the 1986 U.S. immigration law attempts, albeit unsuccessfully, to curtail the international flow of labor. With the ratification of NAFTA, Americans will soon accept the migratory flow of capital. Is it not time that we begin to explore these same possibilities for labor?

Agriculture, a critical sector of the California economy, has for decades acknowledged the need for available and low-wage labor to maintain its competitive position in the domestic and global economy. In every round of immigration reform, agricultural interests have codified their labor market needs through various guest-worker programs. As few American workers in the past forty years have been involved in agricultural production, the successes and failures of these guest-worker programs have remained largely unnoticed, relegated to the expertise of a select number of labor organizers, scholars and political activists. These programs often were faulted for undermining the emergence of a strongly unionized seasonal labor market and undermining harvest workers' wages and working conditions.

Despite the limitations of past guest-worker programs in agriculture, however, they provide a legal framework in which labor-market transactions can occur, elevating underground jobs to a level where public discourse and public policy can truly have an impact on working conditions, wages and employer-employee tax liabilities. For example, guest-worker programs for domestics and child-care providers in Canada provide a legal mechanism for women from the Third World to enter the country, enter the labor market under known conditions and ultimately become citizens.

Guest-worker programs acknowledge that a nation is not an island and that a country's labor needs might not be met by the domestic labor market, despite the well-meaning intentions of those who would like to place the unemployed into guest-worker jobs. Simply increasing wages will not result in a flood of native-born Americans to serve our child-care and other low-wage service-sector needs. Neither will the availability of jobs induce individuals to seek employment where occupational mobility is low. Curtailing immigration by weak attempts to monitor labor markets through employer sanctions and employee verification procedures will not expand the domestic labor market; it will merely increase its distance from the underground economy.

A first step in addressing immigration reform should be to create a policy that places immigrant workers within a legal guest-worker framework in which employers and employees can negotiate wages and working conditions and government's role is to mediate disputes and monitor unfair practices. Second, a bilateral working group representing U.S. and Mexican interests should formulate guidelines for guest-worker programs. Third, U.S. Latinos must add their expertise to the reforms. Finally, labor unions such as the International Ladies Garment Workers and the United Farm Workers—which have targeted undocumented workers in their organizing drives—must work with employers on a collective-bargaining framework. Controlling the flow of illegal-immigrant labor is possible only if there are practical alternatives. Otherwise the underground economy will not only undermine our myopic immigration law, but weaken U.S. labor as the natural forces of a global market operate in the urban core and agricultural fields.

Los Angeles Times Commentary, February 24, 1993

Immigration Reform, Not Hysteria
The SOS initiative would bring immediate court challenges and would take money from strapped public schools.

Here I am promising to write no more letters to the Los Angeles Times *regarding Prop. 187. By itself, 187 cannot do much damage; court cases and restriction will trim it and take much time. If the net effect with Latino citizens is to get them to register and to vote, great! That's what we all want in a democracy.*

—John Andrews

ATTACKS ON undocumented immigrants in California have switched from talk shows to the November ballot, with a proposed law that hopes to exclude these individuals from publicly funded health, education and social-service programs. The "Save Our State" Immigration Initiative (SOS) was spearheaded by Alan Nelson, head of the Immigration and Naturalization Service (INS) in the Reagan Administration, and Harold Ezell, former INS western regional commissioner. The main mechanism that would be used to ensure exclusion from these services would be through legal verification of "suspected" undocumented individuals; providers would be required to report these people to the INS.

This initiative goes beyond limiting entitlements to noncitizens: It violates fundamental rights guaranteed under both the U.S. and California constitutions. For example, the law would force educators and health professionals to violate their legal and ethical standards of confidentiality and their clients' rights of privacy. The initiative attempts to shift the immigration discussion away from employment and toward entitlements. Yet despite the much-ballyhooed studies on the cost of immigrants, there is not a single study that can assert that the main cause of undocumented immigration to the United States is access to entitlements. Rather, most studies suggest that, political upheavals aside, the major pull is higher wages. By ignoring this fundamental influence, the initiative will not stop undocumented immigration.

Another problem with SOS is the lack of data on how much implementing it would cost. A preliminary report from the Senate Office of Research indicates that the state could lose more than $2 billion in federal funds for requiring school districts to report undocumented students to the INS. This loss would be substantially more than the estimated cost of educating the undocumented children. That the proponents of the bill are willing to forgo needed federal dollars for financially strapped public schools suggests that their real agenda is not meaningful immigration reform, but rather to force reform through the courts, using the statute with the specific intent to stimulate further litigation. The authors of the SOS initiative apparently hope to force the Supreme Court to revisit the landmark *Plyer v. Doe* case, which upheld the right of public education for undocumented children in Texas. In that case, Justice William Brennan spoke to the real dangers in a society that would hold children equally culpable for the actions of their parents. The SOS initiative directly contradicts this principle, maintaining equal standards of culpability for children and adults.

These moral concerns aside, it makes no sense to propose a law that would immediately be challenged on constitutional issues, particularly if the impact on undocumented immigration is negligible. In addition, SOS would place school districts at financial risk as they attempt to uphold a state mandate that requires teachers, nurses, social workers, physicians and other service providers to violate their professional codes of ethics to cooperate with the INS.

Californians are more than ready to discuss meaningful immigration reform. This does not mean, however, that we should accept a law that rides on the wave of anti-immigrant hysteria, with neither a solid legal nor financial base. The initiative does not identify where the money for implementation and enforcement will come from, and it specifies no agency for enforcement. Nor does it include any criminal penalties for noncompliance, thereby providing no incentives for compliance. Any thoughtful legislation would have provided these basic pieces of information.

Unfortunately, such flawed and costly initiatives will continue unless Congress and the Clinton Administration tackle reform. In California, the anti-immigrant ideology has become the new litmus test for politicians who hope to appeal to the alienated middle class. These folks have become uncomfortable with the state's new demographic reality and see little help coming from Washington or Sacramento. Their concerns fuel the message of anti-immigrant mavericks—and require our immediate attention if we are to move forward on reform.

Los Angeles Times, July 13, 1994

Many a Slip 'twixt Passage and Enforcement
Even if Prop. 187 survives the courts, its outcome will depend on a new cadre of Latinos in local and state office.

Good or bad as it may be Proposition 187 is a message, not against language, color of skin, not against education or religion. It's first and last A MESSAGE AND REGISTRATION OF OPINION BY THE VOTERS TO LIMIT IMMIGRATION TO THOSE LEGALLY ADMITTED and to send back to point of origin all illegals and their children.
—John Andrews

ON NOV. 9, 1938, Hitler's Nazi regime officially sanctioned the destruction of Jewish shops and synagogues, a major step forward in his drive to solve the "Jewish problem" in Germany. On Nov. 9 of this year, Governor Pete Wilson announced his executive order to immediately enforce provisions of Proposition 187 affecting the health of the most vulnerable of the Latino community, pregnant women and the elderly. Wilson could have waited until the courts clarified the law, but, no longer a moderate, he has acquiesced to the right wing of the Republican Party, which demands not justice but tyranny, which values rhetoric over reason and which seeks to destroy rather than to build.

The Pyrrhic victory of Proposition 187 comes as no surprise to Latinos. Those who remember the ugly political battles over the 1986 Simpson-Mazzoli immigration bill and the English-only movement have learned that when elections become racial, implementation of laws become problematic. Although the state attorney general pledges to fight for 187 up to the U.S. Supreme Court, even he recognized that the resources are not there to challenge the multitude of lawsuits now underway by school districts, professional organizations, and individuals that will whittle away any tangible benefits from this law.

Health professionals, teachers and social workers plan to engage in civil disobedience if asked to enforce provisions of 187. Taxpayers will be stuck paying millions of dollars in litigation costs with no guarantees of successful enforcement but with the certain outcome of dividing a state that can no longer afford to divide. History has demonstrated that the political shelf life of immigration reform is short, even when it is approved by the electorate, as the cost of enforcement soon supersedes any benefits.

The flip side of this white voter backlash against immigrants was the consolidation of a Latino voting bloc that is no longer ambivalent about the legislative agenda of the state's Republican Party. If the Democratic leadership can capture and mobilize this constituency, it could easily become in the next ten years a solid swing vote for Democrats. And unlike the situation in 1986, when California had only a handful of Latino state legislators and congressional representatives, there are more Latino elected officials at every level of government. This growth is not only in traditional

Latino strongholds like Xavier Becerra's 30th congressional District, which includes East Los Angeles, Lucille Roybal-Allard's newly created 33rd District, which includes Huntington Park and South Gate, and Esteban Torres's 34th District, which covers La Puente and Pico Rivera, but also in non-Latino districts such as Assemblyman Joe Baca's 62nd District in San Bernardino County and newly elected Assemblywoman Liz Figueroa's 20th District in the Alameda–Santa Clara area.

That Anglo voters are beginning to cross ethnic lines to vote for Latinos speaks to the real political revolution that 187 proponents choose to ignore: the growth of Latino participation on school boards, city councils and boards of supervisors as well as the state legislature and in Congress. This presence will further challenge Wilson's attempt to enforce a popular but discriminatory law.

There is no doubt that the white electorate still determines the political fate of many Latinos, African Americans and others disenfranchised from our political system. Yet as the state's aging Anglo electorate flexes its muscle once again, it is with an utter detachment from the silent revolution that will continue to grow, not only in the fourteen cities that are more than 70 percent Latino in Los Angeles County, but also throughout the state, where Proposition 187 has galvanized a new generation of Latino voters. And for Anglo voters who speed past the barrios, who choose to ignore the majority of legal Latinos who vote, live and enforce laws in East Los Angeles (95 percent Latino), Huntington Park (92 percent), Bell Gardens (88 percent), Baldwin Park (71 percent) and Lynwood (70 percent): we will be able to prevent enforcement of this racialized law. Even though pundits may dismiss Latinos as nonvoters and passive participants in the political process, their permanent demographic presence in California cannot be denied. Soon Latino voices will be heard across this state.

Los Angeles Times, November 16, 1994

Building Bridges, Not Borders
The United States and Mexico have a compelling mutual interest in addressing problems that know no border.

On the other hand, attention should also be paid to further economic development in the hemisphere. The expansion of NAFTA to include all OAS nations is a step in the right direction.

—*Eduardo Martinez*

FOR MANY AMERICANS, the border with Mexico defines our national sovereignty and identity. It extends almost two thousand miles between four of our southwestern states and six northern Mexican states. Few Americans could name the six—Baja California, Chihuahua, Coahuila, Nuevo Leon, Sonora and Tamaulipas—yet these states increasingly are in our lives.

Recently, I visited Juarez. As I crossed from the United States into Mexico, I realized that there are no meaningful boundaries between these two worlds. More than six hundred million people legally cross the border both ways each year, much to the chagrin of those who would tightly seal every entry point. Those who work, shop and enjoy the comforts of a devalued peso or the luxuries of American goods know all too well the futility of "controlling" such a border.

Today, the border has become the entry point to discuss meaningful binational public policy. As Mexicans migrate in greater numbers to Mexico's industrial north, we will share common space and problems. Our air, water and ecosystems already are part of our binational identity. By 2020, the border region population will have doubled, to 22.8 million, adding greater pressure on scarce natural resources. With this increased population pressure, Mexico and the United States must continue to integrate their regional policy so that a sustained growth is possible without compromising our shared groundwater aquifers, our major desert regions and our valuable rivers and coastlines. Without such strategies, we will suffer the consequences of expanding major environmental hazards beyond California's New River, considered one of the most polluted rivers in the United States, containing toxic industrial waste and at least fifteen deadly viruses such as polio and cholera.

Fortunately, binational partnerships in this region are emerging. Funded by philanthropic organizations like the Ford Foundation and Inter-American Foundation, organizations such as the Comíte Ecológico de Ciudad Juarez, an environmental education and advocacy group, are tackling the pressing problem of environmental contamination in the *maquila,* or duty-free manufacturing and assembly zone. On the Sonora/Arizona border, Enlace Ecológico (the Ecology Connection) has played a critical role in promoting right-to-know legislation on environmental hazards. Similar organizations are developing from Tijuana to Matamoros.

Local binational collaboration also may work on public health issues that have no boundaries. With increased population growth in this region, we also see greater concentration of Third World poverty conditions. On both sides of the border, there are pockets of *colonias,* semirural substandard housing areas where residents have no wastewater treatment or running water. I visited one of these areas on the outskirts of El Paso where 95 percent of the residents tested positive for hepatitis A. A new diagnostic lexicon for doctors in the border region has emerged that includes such diseases as dengue fever, malaria and shigella. Without aggressive binational public health strategies, these diseases may spread throughout the United States.

The border region has a relatively youthful demographic profile and high fertility rate, unlike many regions of the United States, where the reverse is true. So the border area will require educational models that recognize the binational identity of these youth. This goes beyond the issues of Spanish and English fluency to the broader issue of a shared educational and cultural experience by border dwellers.

Recently, philanthropic organizations on both sides of the border met in Juarez to discuss philanthropy and shared funding strategies for border issues. Rejecting the rhetoric of nationalism and isolationism, the philanthropic community has taken an important step in shifting the American debate on the border. By ignoring the popular anti-immigrant trend, these organizations have infused the discussion with a reality where across communities lines in the sand have little meaning and visions for change build bridges—not borders across communities.

Los Angeles Times, June 12, 1996

Immigration Revisited: Issues in the Twenty-First Century

During the 1990s, many of the issues that framed the immigration debates in California were politicized due to the visible demographic shift in this state as well as the economic recession that plagued California during the early part of the decade. The combined impact of the "browning" of California with the decline of the high-paying manufacturing jobs in the aerospace industry, for example, provided the perfect political opportunity for Governor Pete Wilson to exploit the emotional vulnerabilities of an insecure electorate.

Despite the recognition by large segments of the business community that immigrant labor, particularly Latino workers, played critical roles in the California economy, the emerging identity crisis of the California electorate dominated the political agenda of the 1990s. Moreover, the Latino political representation lay primarily within single-member (minority) districts. That is, Latino state legislators, congressional representatives, and local elected officials were in districts that were disproportionately Latino. For example, cities such as Huntington Park, which has a population base at least 90 percent Latino, elected mayors and city council members who were predominately Latino. With the exception of Gloria Molina, who became the first Latina and woman to be elected to the L.A. County Board of Supervisors in 1991 after the Mexican American Legal Defense and Education Fund (MALDEF) filed a lawsuit against L.A. County for violating the federal Voting Rights Act in 1990, political representation was largely segregated by ethnicity in mostly Latino enclaves.[1]

The key issues facing the emerging Latino community during the 1990s were:

1. Immigrant rights regarding access to public services, particularly the impact of differential access by legal and illegal immigrants to these services
2. NAFTA, which divided the Latino community into those with pro-union views versus those with pro–free trade and pro-Mexico perspectives
3. The unwillingness of legislators to develop a proactive strategy in addressing immigrant labor market policies and entitlements programs
4. The racialization of the immigrant issues as ideologically defined by the impact of recent Mexican immigration.

Immigrant Rights

Perhaps no other issue dominated the political landscape for Mexican immigrants in California more than Proposition 187. This state initiative curtailed health care, education and public services for illegal immigrants and became symbolic of the anti-immigrant rhetoric of the 1990s. The so-called "Save Our State" initiative was developed by Harold Ezell, former INS western regional commissioner during the Reagan Administration, and promoted by then Governor Pete Wilson. Proposition 187 began the political discourse of separating Mexicans and Mexican Americans from the broader political electorate. It did so first by linking an ethnic phenotype, i.e., Mexicans, to a stereotype that characterized Mexicans as excessively using welfare and other public service programs. Although documented evidence proved the contrary, Wilson successfully played on nativist fears of the growing shift in political power away from the existing white electorate to a growing minority electorate. Ironically, this fear was not generated by actual political participation of Mexican immigrants, but rather by the visual demographic shift within southern California and the social landscape.

It is not surprising that anti-Mexican fears were easily fueled by the rhetoric of Wilson and his allies given the historical political success of targeting immigrants during periods of economic duress. Because Mexican immigrants have historically been marginalized through federal, state and local policies that allowed for educational segregation, economic isolation and easy methods of deporting them, this pattern of political scapegoating has been widely accepted and used by white politicians.[2] Thus, the institutional racism experienced by the Mexican-origin population over several decades in California provided the backdrop for understanding the persistence of hostility toward this group, even when it was not the cause of the overall deterioration of California's economy or its social fabric.

In response to the growing influx of Mexican immigrants to California, the Clinton Administration increased the level of border suppression of illegal immigrants through programs such as "Operation Gatekeeper," which was implemented in San Diego County in 1994. Thus, even with a more "sympathetic" Democratic administration, the strategy of control was to militarize the border region and thereby stem the flow of Mexican immigrants. In addition, the federal government's role in defending entitlements for both legal and illegal immigrants has not significantly improved in light of the new welfare reforms. Prior to final negotiations with the Hispanic Caucus, there was a real threat that even legal immigrants would be excluded from entitlement programs such as Medicaid and Supplemental Security Income (SSI) for the elderly and disabled. Thus, federal policies became less inclusive during the latter part of the 1990s with respect to immigrants and integration of this group through established social welfare policies in California.

Since the 1990s the underlying hostility toward Mexican immigrants appears to have softened. Yet, during the 1990s, federal and state policies fostered an environment in which inclusion of more recent immigrants within the social and economic institutions became more difficult. This is immediately apparent when we look beyond the more recent issue of increased political participation of Latinos in the California electorate. For example, we see the increasing gap in educational attainment between non-Latinos and Latino immigrants, the overrepresentation of Latinos in both adult and juvenile corrections, and the growing economic disparity between the poor Latino immigrants and more established Latino and non-Latino households. Thus, as we enter the twenty-first century, the prospects for economic advancement are more difficult for Latino immigrants because of the overall shift in labor market forces and the decline of federal and state support for integrating immigrants rapidly into the U.S. economy.

NAFTA

In addition to the proliferation of immigrant bashing during the 1990s in California, there was a simultaneous drive to increase free trade within the Western Hemisphere. No other policy captured the shifting power dynamics within the U.S. economy as did the North American Free Trade Agreement (NAFTA). As technological markets and financial markets opened up the world economy beyond domestic borders, the need to remove barriers to trade became a central goal of the Clinton Administration.

The NAFTA debate juxtaposed with the anti-immigrant rhetoric posed an interesting dilemma for the Clinton Administration, as it tried to balance its free trade agenda with more restrictive policies for immigrants living in the United States. Both the U.S. and Mexican governments actively supported this trinational trade initiative with the hopes of further stimulating Mexico's economic growth as well as benefiting the U.S. and Canadian economies. Within the context of the broader U.S. Latino community, NAFTA was overwhelmingly supported by the Hispanic Caucus and widely recognized within the Latino business community as providing greater market opportunities for Latino entrepreneurs. Although there were vocal Latino critics in the Southwest and California, these individuals were tied to the traditional trade unions that were anti-NAFTA. However, they represented a small portion of the Latino community, particularly if one considers those living in the border regions who viewed NAFTA as a potential boon to their regional economies. Thus, NAFTA provided a cross-ethnic policy that generated mutual political support from both Latino as well as non-Latino communities.

Nonetheless, underlying the pro-market and pro–economic development rhetoric of NAFTA lurked the negative stereotypes of

Mexicans as enemies of the American way of life. Independents like Ross Perot and conservative, racist politicians like Pat Buchanan attributed job loss and deterioration in American quality of life to Mexican workers. Although trade unionists were less caustic in their characterizations of Mexican workers, the paternalistic tone of much of the union literature diminished the capacity of Mexicans to protect their own work force from capitalist exploitation. That jobs would be lost because of NAFTA was a valid concern of both trade unionists and workers in blue-collar industries. However, the economic dynamic of more open trade already existed under the policies that former Mexican President Carlos Salinas de Gortari established to open up Mexico markets to the global economy in the late 1980s and early 1990s. The impact of anti-NAFTA efforts was mitigated by the preexisting internal free trade policies within Mexico that set the stage for the final formalization of the treaty.

Immigrants and NAFTA were linked within the context of the demonization of Mexicans and their supposed challenge to American culture and standards of living. This demonization was in direct contradiction to the reality that immigrants produce the wealth that underpins the American economy. This contradiction remains as Americans still are uncomfortable with the greater regional economic interdependency between Mexico and the United States, which, given the rapid population growth on the Mexican side of the border, will only increase. With the newly elected conservative Partido Acción Nacional (PAN) president, Vicente Fox, there will be even greater economic growth in Mexico and increased cooperation between the two countries. Both presidents Bush and Fox share a vision of greater economic integration and expanded trade between Mexico and the United States.

Labor Market Policy

In California, the idea of developing a proactive labor market policy for immigrants has fallen to the wayside because of the overwhelming influence of the manufacturing, agricultural, and service sector interests. Historically, Mexican-origin workers in the Southwest have filled low-wage-sector jobs such as in agriculture, with the assistance of federal and state policies that allowed a steady flow of low-wage workers. These policies effectively prevented long-term unionization due to the constant availability of low-wage immigrant labor. Moreover, if unionization is not sustainable or possible in a given sector, there is little motivation by employers to improve wages or working conditions for these workers. Even as we enter the twenty-first century, there have been no effective labor market solutions to address the use of both immigrant and illegal workers in the low-wage employment sectors.

Solutions such as those mentioned in my earlier commentaries relating to higher payroll taxes on employers that disproportionately employ undocumented workers, providing funds to monitor industries where the abuse of both immigrant and illegal labor may occur, or developing targeted guest-worker programs are not politically feasible. However, without effective labor market policies focused on support services for low-wage workers, or limiting worker access to industries that are unwilling to cover the costs of providing these services, abuse of immigrant Latinos will continue.

Immigrant labor market policy solutions are difficult to address for the Latino leadership as well as for employers who use these workers, because of conflicting issues surrounding these proposed solutions. For Latinos, the negative memory of the Bracero Program (1942–1964) creates enormous ambivalence about any labor market policy that suggests the use of a guest-worker program, even when potential conditions could be improved for these workers. An example of this is the challenge by Latino groups of the proposal developed by Arizona Governor Jane Hull, where the fear of a Bracero-like program was resurrected in the political discourse.

Policies that restrict immigrant labor from Mexico also create tensions within the Latino community, because of concern over the use of racial profiling. Thus, labor supply policies that either enhance the flow of immigrant labor, such as guest-worker programs, or restrict the flow, such as limiting immigrant groups based on quotas, continue to create political unease and discord within the Latino community. However, many Latinos in Arizona, for example, argue that the appalling conditions faced by undocumented immigrants who cross the treacherous Sonoran Desert and are exploited by smugglers known as "coyotes" is far worse than a guest-worker program. As tensions and problems escalate, the presence of violent drug cartels and unscrupulous coyotes are just part of the problem. The prospect of a guest-worker program becomes increasingly appealing to Latinos living in the border region.

For the non-Latino community, opinions on immigrant labor issues are divided between employers who rely on these workers and private citizens who fear labor market competition, which may affect their standard of living. These competing interests reflect the historical struggle for power between organized labor and employers in shaping immigration policy. Agricultural interests have long been favored, as illustrated by laws such as the National Origins Act of 1924, which established a quota system based on national origin; the National Labor Relations Act (1935); and the Immigration Reform and Control Act (IRCA) of 1986, which preserved the favored status of agricultural employers who relied on cheap Mexican labor.[3] Recently, these issues have become more politicized, as the increased demographic presence of Latinos in states like California has created an additional tension, as witnessed in the debates on Proposition 187.

Ideology

Beyond the political and economic realities of the 1990s that fostered anti-immigrant sentiments, there was an overriding ideological shift among politicians and private citizens that supported overt demonization of Mexican immigrants. This was fostered by the media not only in its political coverage, but also in its political support of racist politicians. For example, the *Los Angeles Times'* support of Governor Pete Wilson during the 1994 gubernatorial election provided the platform for his continued use of racial politics in defining California's public policy issues. Proposition 187 is an excellent example of how to put inflammatory and divisive rhetoric to good use in a political campaign. Even Democratic Senator Dianne Feinstein used derogatory images of Mexican immigrants running across the U.S.-Mexico border in her television campaign ads during this period to solidify the moderate white vote within her constituency, illustrating that these tactics had no party boundaries.

Notes

1. Rodolfo F. Acuña, *Anything But Mexican: Chicanos in Contemporary Los Angeles* (London and New York: Verso, 1996), 43–75.

2. During the 1930s and again in 1954 ("Operation Wetback"), hundreds of Mexicans and Mexican Americans were deported to Mexico, because Americans believed they posed a threat to the U.S. economy as public charges during times of severe economic depression. For more information on the repatriation and deportation of Mexican-origin people, see Francisco E. Balderrama, *Mexican Repatriation in the 1930s* (Albuquerque: University of New Mexico Press, 1995); Juan R. Garcia, *Operation Wetback: The Mass Deportation of Mexican Undocumented Workers in 1954* (Westport, Conn.: Greenwood Press, 1980); and Abraham Hoffman, *Unwanted Mexican Americans in the Great Depression: Repatriation Pressures, 1929–1939* (Tucson: University of Arizona Press, 1974).

3. David Gutiérrez, *Walls and Mirrors: Mexican Americans, Mexican Immigrants, and the Politics of Ethnicity* (Berkeley and Los Angeles: University of California Press, 1995), 43–53, 105.

CHAPTER 2

ISSUES IN
BILINGUAL
AND K–12
EDUCATION

Seeing the Future in the Classroom
If the next generation is to succeed, today's adults must renew and
revitalize our urban public schools.

I'm writing partially to let you know I was very impressed by your column

"Language Is a Bridge to Culture" on the bilingual-education issue [which]

appeared in today's Los Angeles Times. *It was very human, rather than*

the usual whining and/or hate-mongeral [sic] *that appear on both sides.*

. . . I know there have always been enclaves of probably every ethnic group

that has immigrated to the U.S. But I think the general opinion of the

European-origin citizen is that Hispanics—generally perceived Mexican

in the Southwest—are unique in wanting the U.S. to adapt to them rather

than embracing the language and culture of what is supposed to be their

new country. I'm sure the proximity of Mexico contributes, but it's irri-

tating to hear people who've lived in the U.S. most of their lives referring

*to themselves as Mexicans rather than Americans and waving Mexican
flags in political demonstrations. This only leads to divisiveness.*
—Thomas Erskine

*I do not feel that it is my responsibility to give a sense of tradition; that
should be to the parents. Where do you draw the line at Spanish, Korean,
Russian, Hebrew, Iranian? Maybe we should just have individual instruction for every language.*
—William Ash

EACH YEAR I look forward to spending a day visiting my daughter's
school, to get a snapshot of her life in our local middle school and
thereby have a better sense of both her accomplishments and her
frustrations. More recently, my motives shifted to include a broader
dimension of concern: How well will these seventh-graders fare in
the year 2001 if the California State University system begins to
screen entry based on math and English writing skills?

My daughter warned me not to expect too much from her
classes, that boredom was a common complaint among her peers.
The monotonous ebb and flow of the classes, she said, changed
only when there was an ingenuous substitute teacher. At best, the
substitutes attempt to review old assignments while maintaining a
semblance of class order; more often, the sub ends up as a baby-
sitter with a video. As I listened to my daughter's caricatures of the
substitutes, I realized that she and her friends were paying a price
for not having a teacher who cared whether they learned something
that day.

As I walked the halls following my daughter's daily rotation, I
saw the sea of faces that defines our urban public schools. Two-
thirds of her classmates are Latino, African American or Asian.
One in four is limited in English proficiency and one in four is poor.
This environment explains why many professional parents opt out

of urban public schools: to protect their children from the harsh reality of the growing divide in American society.

As I visited each class, I noticed an interesting pattern emerging. There were those instructors whose thematic core was to establish some semblance of order and discipline in the classroom void of any real content. Perhaps the best example of this was a physical education instructor who barked orders and used public humiliation to modify unruly student behavior. There were other classrooms where the issue of discipline was secondary, and the content of the curriculum was present immediately after the bell rang. This was best illustrated by an algebra teacher who directly challenged his students to review a recent exam and redo those problems marked wrong. In time the moans and groans subsided, as the children slapped their foreheads in disbelief when they realized their own careless mistakes. I saw the glow emanate from their faces once they began to gain control of their own learning.

Yet even with the best teachers, I saw the insurmountable odds that our urban schools must face today. In my daughter's English class, the students were assigned to read and prepare for a test. A young man was asked to read aloud a section from O. Henry's "The Gift of the Magi." As he stumbled over every other word, I couldn't help but wonder if the struggle to sound out the words hampered his ability to understand them. After the class, I spoke with the teacher. There were exceptions in the class, she said, and the curriculum allowed for the expansion of a student's individual potential, but how far could she go when many of her seventh-graders hovered at best at a fourth-grade reading level? This made me realize that the issue of remediation will not go away by the year 2001.

As parents, educators and business leaders, we have accepted with little protest that California is now thirty-eighth in the nation in per capita spending in public education, and we are now ranked in last place both in reading scores and class size. We have not been serious about preparing our students for the next century.

As an educator, I want a seamless system where children naturally progress from one tier of education to another. As a parent, I want what is best for my child: an education that challenges her potential and rewards her creativity. And as a community member,

I want the best public school system so that our youth may enter the career paths of their choice and so employers view them as part of a successful business future. As we leave the twentieth century, one measure of its success should be the renewal of our public schools so that all our children may share in our loyalties and our dreams.

Los Angeles Times, January 17, 1996

False Figure Fuels Furor
A tax on employers who hire illegals could be used to subsidize the schools that educate their children.

I would like to ask you to consider the fact that undocumented workers pay more than their fair share of taxes already in the form of sales taxes. The working poor are more likely to spend a larger proportion of their incomes on basic necessities than do middle and upper class members of a [sic] communities. Recent studies by the Tomás Rivera Policy Institute at Claremont College and the Lyndon B. Johnson School of Public Policy at the University of Texas have shown that undocumented workers add to overall economies rather that drain public revenues. I argue that funds should be diverted from current tax revenues to cover the cost of the education of the undocumented children rather than create new taxes.
—Eduardo Martinez

THE DEBATE over providing public education to children of undocumented immigrants centers on the "$2-billion subsidy" borne by California taxpayers. Those who quote this expense assume that it is the true cost of educating these children and will be the net savings to the public education system from barring illegal immigrants. As an economist, my curiosity is piqued by the underlying assumptions used to construct this number.

The basis for the $2-billion estimate comes from projections by the Immigration and Naturalization Service and the Census Bureau. Using these data, a common estimate for the number of undocumented children enrolled in California public schools is about three hundred thousand. This number is then multiplied by the per pupil average costs, which for large urban school districts have ranged between six thousand and seven thousand dollars a year.

The problem with this estimate, however, is not the number of undocumented children enrolled in public schools, but the use of average cost data rather than marginal cost data—that is, the additional costs of educating the undocumented students. This is a major methodological flaw. Average costs include fixed costs such as buildings, debt payment on bonds and in some instances, multiyear negotiated contracts for salaried employees and variable costs such as classroom materials and supplies. In the case of K–12 education, there is a considerable amount of fixed cost hidden in the average cost estimate and a limited amount of variable cost. Therefore, eliminating access to K–12 education to undocumented students will not result in a $2-billion cost savings. The fixed costs of these school districts will remain. So the closings and teacher layoffs required to save this amount of money will not happen, because these fixed costs are required to meet the needs of the remaining students.

So what does this supposed $2-billion savings really mean? We can at best use it as a political red flag and hope that the federal government responds by providing us with more resources. As for the incremental impact of immigrant students, researchers have begun to sort out some of the additional costs to targeted programs like bilingual education. A preliminary study under way by the Urban Institute suggests that the incremental cost to the core curriculum for bilingual education may be only one thousand dollars per pupil. Using this approach would drastically reduce our cost estimate from $2 billion to $300 million or less.

With meaningful marginal cost estimates, we could then shift the cost burden to the real culprits involved in the undocumented migration flow: employers. Rather than making educational access the issue in immigration control, we could use the marginal cost estimates to develop targeted taxes to employers who hire undocumented workers. This incremental tax would be based on the number of projected undocumented employees. The tax would be applied across the board in an industry such as farming or garment manufacture, with individual employers granted exemptions if they can certify the status of their employees. The new tax would go to the local school district.

The beauty of using the tax system instead of the educational system as one mechanism for controlling immigration is that it targets where the hidden subsidy is and transfers that subsidy to where the real cost is borne. It reduces the cost for enforcement of immigration law from the government to the private sector. In sum, this is not only a better strategy for controlling the flow of undocumented immigrants, but also a way to shift the responsibility squarely where it belongs: on employers who choose to hire undocumented employees.

Los Angeles Times, July 31, 1996

Voucher Opponents Miss the Point
Decrying as elitist parents' desire for quality and safety in education does little to advance the public school cause.

The question becomes, "What should the taxpayers expect from public education?" . . . if the answer is to create a society where all citizens have an equal opportunity to achieve their goals and dreams, then it seems to me our responsibility is to provide them with the necessary tools. In the United States this means English language skills and a rigorous academic schedule. Surely the immigrants who came to this country over the two centuries since its founding expected as much.

—Dave Walters

The tone of your column makes you sound like someone to whom I can pose thoughts and questions you might address in future columns. From my perspective, the articles, columns, and letters-to-the-editor I've seen

over the decades on the Latino issues in general have been very uninfor-

mative and frustrating in trying to understand "the other side." While I

don't presume to speak for the entire European-origin population of the

United States, I am sure my perceptions are not unique. By the way, when

I use the word "you" I don't mean you personally. It's a shorthand for

addressing what might be considered the stereotype Hispanic/Mexican

activist. . . . In the political arena, phrases like "sensitive to the needs of

Hispanics" often appear. Yet these "needs" are never specified. What do

"the Hispanics" need from the various levels of government that's differ-

ent from the rest of us?

—*Thomas Erskine*

PROPOSITION 174, the school-voucher initiative, has become a lightning rod for discussion among educators across the nation. As the fiscal crisis facing public education grows, the threat of further funding cuts erodes a system in which teacher and student needs continue to be undermined. Yet the campaign to stop this proposition has coalesced groups across the political spectrum in a strategy that plays on the fears of parents that Proposition 174 is not only anti–public school, but also an entitlement program for the rich. Unfortunately, in this drive to stop 174, we have missed the opportunity to address an important issue that has plagued the hearts of working- and middle-class parents: access to quality education for their children in a safe environment.

For many Mexican Americans and African Americans, the issue of quality has forced re-evaluation of their commitment to public education. In the heart of Los Angeles or New York, the local parochial schools are filled with black and brown faces. That many parents in the urban core opt out of public education is not surprising, given the real fears that their children will not learn in an environment plagued with violence and with peer groups that negate the family values that they struggle to infuse in their children. Many working parents merely want their children to have a sanctuary for learning where common codes of behavior are assumed and teachers are not distracted from teaching. This is why, despite the economic hardship, many of these parents choose parochial schools—not because they do not believe in public education, but because they are not willing to gamble their children's future to prove that the system works. As I reflect back on my own mother's choice to place my sister and me in a local parish school more than thirty years ago, I realize how personal Proposition 174 has become for many voters. As a single parent and public school teacher, my mother valued her colleagues, but knew that, given where we lived, I would not have a secure environment for learning in public school.

I remember little of the agonizing emotional and financial choice my mother made for her children. What I do remember is learning the art of using mass transit and growing up with hand-me-down green pleated skirts and white saddle shoes that always left a trail of white powder as I walked. I remember envying the stylish young girls walking up the street with their miniskirts and go-go boots while I languished in Peter Pan collars and oversized sweaters. As the middle-school years approached, I pleaded with my mother to let me go to the local junior high school so that I could become a normal girl. She honored my request and let me attend summer school in the public school, where more often than not I would become the teachers' pet because they knew I was there to learn. Although from my point of view I fared well in both the public and private settings, my mother would never waver in her choice for our education. Years later, I asked my mother why she didn't let us go to public schools, and her reply still rings true: "You were the only children I would have in my lifetime and I was unwilling to sacrifice you for any cause, even a cause I believe in."

It is not surprising that emotion will often transcend reason with our children. But when parental emotion is linked to real fears—fears that make parents instinctively act to preserve any safety net for their children—then rhetoric that points to financial disaster or uncertainty in public education has minimal impact. Public educators who ignore or dismiss these real fears as racist or anti–public school will lose not only an important opportunity for dialogue, but also a powerful constituency that would work with them for effective change. Parents who care about their children and education are worth listening to, even if their voices do not echo those of the established power brokers.

To ignore the roots of why Proposition 174 is on the ballot and not engage in an honest debate of why it crosses racial, ethnic and class lines is to lose an opportunity to assess the shortcomings of our system and create an alternative vision of public education for our children. Despite its limitations, Proposition 174 speaks to real fears of parents that must be addressed by public education. Be assured that these fears will not dissipate after November's election.

Los Angeles Times, October 20, 1993

Perspective on Bilingual Education

Language Is a Bridge to Culture
Latinos' ambivalence toward Proposition 227 comes from the suspicion that it is an attempt to obliterate their heritage.

Whose responsibility is it to teach the language and culture of the home country? Certainly not the state or the taxpayers of the state. It is a home responsibility. The state should not condemn their efforts, nor should they [sic] have to pay for it!

—Dave Walters

I just wanted to thank you for writing such an insightful piece. I agree wholeheartedly with the points that you raised and find myself surprised at the impassioned conflict that this issue raises here in California. When my mother taught my sisters and I to speak as infants, she taught us both languages at the same time. As a "Nuyorican," I have never visited Puerto Rico, but my Spanish-speaking abuelita was an important part of our

family and my mother wanted us to communicate with her. Like you, my
fluency needs some work, but it's been strong enough to make me valuable
in the job market. . . . Why bilingualism is such a threat to non-Latinos is
a mystery to me. After all, when the wealthy send their children to study
abroad, they see to it that they learn other languages. These children are
considered lucky to have such a well-rounded education. We, on the other
hand, were born close enough to our culture that we don't have to pay
thousands to learn the language yet we are considered crippled (as one
teacher called me) for speaking it.

—Rosemary Rivera-Menjivar

I REMEMBER WELL the magic of knowing two languages as a child. My maternal grandmother, an immigrant from the heart of central Mexico, raised me with the certainty that mastering the language of her adopted country would only bring greater opportunities. Although I rarely quibbled with my grandmother, I knew that with the warmth of our home language—our *dichos* (sayings) and *canciones* (songs)—I could begin to understand who I was and who I would become.

If there are two aspects of my childhood that I remember best, it is my home language, Spanish, and my religion, Catholicism. Language and religion were not mutually exclusive activities in my life. They were so intertwined that even when I entered the monolingual parochial schools, I would never end my rosary without the Spanish prayer of "Dulce Madre" (Sweet Mother). Somehow, I felt that without including this prayer in my rosary, the Virgin would not hear my pleas. How could the detached, mournful drone of a "Hail Mary" compete with the lyrical sweetness of a child's prayer that asked for a mother's constant vigilance? It was obvious to me then and now that the dominant culture could have meaning in my eyes only with remnants of my family language.

Over time, I learned to weave my home language into my new life. I chose never to abandon my home language; rather, I learned that Spanish allowed me to stay rooted to my grandmother's vision as I transformed myself into a new mestiza.

Although I never attained the level of Spanish fluency that I desired, I continued my grandmother's tradition of maintaining our home language with my own daughters. My goal was less focused on the notion of fluency than on ensuring that they would maintain some semblance of a distinct Mexican cultural identity. Understanding Spanish would provide them not only with a link to our roots, but also with an entry point to traversing more than one culture. How they will view my efforts as adult women is hard to tell. Yet like many Latinas, I tried, at least symbolically, to maintain our language as well as our customs.

Oddly, when we speak of bilingual education, we forget the symbolism of what language means to individuals. When my non-Latino colleagues ask me about bilingual education, they expect a rational economist's response. I've often heard remarks that go something like: "Well, the numbers tell the story, don't they? The situation is getting worse for Mexican Americans and you've had ample time to prove your point with bilingual education." Or, "Look at you, you were never in bilingual education and you were successful." The discussion then inevitably shifts to transition rates into English, the number of kids with limited English, the correlation between English proficiency and income and job mobility and, of course, the alarming Latino dropout rates.

Truth be told, we can play with all these numbers and conjure up any story we want to believe about bilingual education. Leaving aside the debate over which are the relevant numbers and studies, we still may find several consensus points. For example, we could probably agree on the fact that bilingual education is just one among many educational programs that have had problems. We also may agree that there is a dire need for reform (and sufficient funding) in K–12 education and a need for explicit measures that can clearly assess student performance in all programs and subjects.

We also know that most surveys of Latinos illustrate a strong desire that their children become fluent in English. Yet these same surveys often illustrate some ambivalence toward attacks on bilingual education. Why do Latinos exhibit such contradictory attitudes? One response illustrates the clear understanding of the need to become fluent in English to attain economic and political power. The other response illustrates an unwillingness to reject an educational policy that was created to help Latinos. Perhaps this latter is best explained in the context of our unwillingness to completely cede our identity to a dominant culture that has viewed us as marginal.

In many ways, maintaining our language is a final act of resistance—a resistance that increasingly is fueled by the racism that is manifest in popular culture as well as popular initiatives like Proposition 187 and more recently in Proposition 227, the so-called Unz Initiative. Language never will be a simple binary issue for most Latinos. This becomes even more apparent when opponents of bilingual education code their message in racial terms. Despite attempts to make bilingual education a more general issue, it is viewed by many Latinos as a language rights issue. This inevitably strikes at the heart of how we view ourselves. Across generations, we struggle to maintain some continuity with our roots, and those roots are deeply embedded in our language.

Can there be a rational dialogue on bilingual education? Certainly there are points of compromise and room for discussion. Yet within the shadows of this policy debate is the soul of our identity. And this shadow will continue to filter the lens through which Latinos view bilingual education and how we measure those who oppose it. A clear example of this occurred when noted educator Jaime Escalante publicly joined the campaign for the Unz Initiative. In many Latino circles, he was vilified as a traitor. Certainly that is an irrational response, but it shows clearly that some Latinos are not convinced of the sincerity of the non-Latino electorate's goals for our economic and political assimilation.

The problem with Proposition 227 is that it forces us into a zero-sum choice. Learning English is important for all Latinos and is not incompatible with maintaining our Spanish. As with the rest of public instruction, we need to have specific standards of instruction, we need to have specific standards of performance for bilingual programs and take into account parents' preferences. The strategy should not be to eliminate bilingual education but to take what's best in these programs and incorporate them into our public schools.

Until Latinos have confidence that attacks on bilingual education are truly targeted on helping our assimilation and not on erasing our identity, there will be little middle ground for reasoned discourse, as language will remain a symbol of our defiance.

Los Angeles Times, March 22, 1998

Reflections on the Debates in K–12 during the Twenty-First Century

Bilingual education, equal education opportunity, educational standards, and Spanish language retention are themes that have transcended the 1990s and are ever present in the discourse of the current century. In many respects the debate over bilingual education in California during the 1990s set the stage for these debates outside of California. For example, the present "English for the Children" initiative (Proposition 203) to end bilingual education in Arizona can be directly linked to the success of Proposition 227 (the so-called Unz Initiative), which eliminated mandatory bilingual education programs in California. Although many Mexican American parents who oppose bilingual education for their children heavily support the initiative, significant support and assistance for the Arizona initiative came primarily from Ron Unz and his California supporters.

The issue of bilingual education in the Southwest has been plagued by controversy from its inception. This controversy is rooted in the historical segregation based on linguistic and cultural "deficiencies" as well as ethnicity evident in cases like the 1930 Lemon Grove Incident in San Diego, where school officials built a separate school for Mexican children that was clearly inferior in construction and teaching materials to the school for whites. That same year, the League of United Latin American Citizens (LULAC) won its first lawsuit against school officials in Del Rio, Texas, in *Salvatierra v. Independent School District.* The case resulted in the elimination of discriminatory educational practices against Mexican Americans. These episodes establish the historical legacy of educational discrimination against Mexican American children that remain bitter memories for many. Historical segregation in American schools based on language and ethnicity had devastatingly reduced educational and economic opportunities for generations of Mexican Americans. The combination of historical segregation as well as the symbolic importance of language and culture in the formation of ethnic identity has had long-lasting effects on how the Latino community, particularly the Mexican American community, has responded to attacks on bilingual education.

It must be made clear from the onset in the political discourse on bilingual education that this debate should center on the pedagogy of using Spanish as a tool in bridging the transition to English instruction, not on the "Americanization" of Latinos.[1]

Another important issue during the 1990s was the quality of education within minority communities. The charter school movement grew and the voucher program, which shifted public dollars to private schools, appeared attractive in response to the perceived deterioration of public schools. This quality issue resulted in the unsuccessful voucher initiative drive in California known as Proposition 174. Communities within inner city low-income districts where academic performance of minority students was deteriorating were important targets in these campaigns, as student performance was linked to the quality of instruction in inner city public schools. In my commentary about Proposition 174, I expressed my ambivalence, a reaction shared by many Latino professionals as well as working-class parents. Given the choice between bad public schools and better quality private schools such as parochial schools, most Latino parents will opt for private schools if they are provided with vouchers. It is well established that parochial schools provide excellent educational opportunities for minority students, which translates into greater economic opportunity for these children. However, a large percentage of Latinos support public education as indicated by a July 2000 Knight-Ridder Poll.

During the last presidential election, the voucher initiative resurfaced in California with Proposition 34, but once again failed to garner the support of the California electorate. President Bush also supported the voucher strategy at a federal level, but as of yet, has not been able to garner adequate congressional support to include vouchers as a viable federal educational policy.

The dilemma faced by the Latino leadership, which is largely Democratic, is the need to maintain consistency with a pro–public school stance while recognizing that vouchers are a viable alternative when public schools fail. Although the most recent voucher initiative failed in California, it symbolizes the potential schism between the Latino political leadership and many Latino parents who are concerned that educational policies may serve the more liberal agenda of the Democratic Party at the price of an inferior educational system for their children.

To date, the demands for better quality education for Latino children have not been met by the public education system. Without significant reform, this may create further educational problems for our children. This does not mean that public schools cannot serve our children, but it implies that to correct past inequalities, we must begin an honest dialogue among school officials, parents, and elected officials about why the current system has failed. Without improving educational outcomes for low-income minority students in public schools, the voucher initiative will continue to attract dissatisfied parents whose children are not well served in local public schools.

Educational reforms such as voucher initiatives, charter schools, standardized tests, and school restructuring all share common themes. These include the following:

- Accountability to children and parents within the public system based on performance
- Equal opportunity for quality education through increased market competition within the K–12 system
- Negative financial consequences for schools, administrators and teachers that fail to meet standards in educating children

In sum, the issues that were articulated with considerable debate during the 1990s are still fresh in the minds of the electorate—both Latino and non-Latino. Perhaps this is of even greater significance to the Latino community, as school performance indicators point to continued inequality and high drop-out rates within the Latino population, particularly in the Southwest. A recent

Harvard study suggests there is hypersegregation, that is, an increasing segregation of Latino students in public schools resulting in a wider educational gap between Latino and non-Latino students.

A final recurring theme in the 1990s was the financing of public education for undocumented students, which surfaced with the Republican Party's debates surrounding Proposition 187. Although this immigration-related issue was an important one, its significance in California was eventually overshadowed by more pressing issues such as the drug trade, vigilante action and human rights violations against Mexican immigrants in the border region. Despite the negative impact of the heated debates over undocumented immigration, the positive impact of a more robust economy in the Southwest has reduced the importance of using a strategy based on scapegoating in the political arena. Moreover, with a newly elected Democratic California governor and legislature, it is highly unlikely that immigrant bashing, particularly that of immigrant children, will resurface in the California political debates during the next ten years.

Note

1. For information on the segregation of Mexican Americans in the public schools see Guadalupe San Miguel, *"Let All of Them Take Heed": Mexican Americans and the Campaign for Educational Equality in Texas, 1910–1981* (Austin: University of Texas Press, 1987) and Gilbert G. González, *Chicano Education in the Era of Segregation* (Philadelphia: Balch Institute Press, 1990).

CHAPTER 3

ISSUES IN
HIGHER
EDUCATION

Rethinking Higher Education
Tenure, campus autonomy, unfettered research—these may be ideas whose time has passed in California.

Thanks for your excellent critique of higher education in the Times *today. I hope we can work together on reform—it's almost too late.*

—Tom Hayden

Thank you for speaking out in your great article in yesterday's Los Angeles Times. *As a retired teacher of adults in the Los Angeles Schools, I felt that I must write you to say "Amen." . . . You are so right about "the painful academic process" that can be made more palatable by competent teachers. Rote learning and computers are so much easier for lazy academics. Right?*

—Mary Meyer

AS THE CALIFORNIA DEFICIT continues to soar, so does the crisis in public higher education. Top administrators from the University of California (UC), California State University (CSU) and the community colleges continue to wring their hands about the impending impact of last years cuts. Tenured faculty who in the past were immune from the vicissitudes of sporadic economizing are beginning to recognize that even their feudal hierarchy of fiefdoms may not survive the wrath of management's budget-tightening measures. Students well aware of the uncertainty rush to meet course requirements for graduation before the next announcement of a 40 percent fee hike.

For decades, California had been on the cutting edge of higher education—a model of affordability and access. Students were charged nominal fees, not the exorbitant tuition of private institutions such as Stanford, to allow for the best and the brightest of the state to become the rising stars of industry, medicine and education. Yet with last year's round of budget cuts, this model has rapidly degenerated, so that access and affordability may become mutually exclusive goals for future generations of college students. This shift toward closing the doors to qualified students in public higher education comes at a time when the public rhetoric strongly advocates the need for a more competitive work force and the public high school population is increasingly Latino and Asian.

Most observers recognize that despite the obvious need to support public higher education today, the political and economic reality is that it is insignificant compared with other pressing state needs such as health care and public primary and secondary education. Most likely, severe cuts will require further reductions in course offerings for students and research opportunities for faculty. But before we allow the continued mutilation of academic programs by technocratic drones who have rarely entered a classroom or research laboratory, it is critical that faculty and administrators develop a strategic plan for higher education for the twenty-first century.

If the goal is to be on the cutting edge of higher education, it is critical that we devise a plan that not only provides quality, but also is cost effective. A first step would be to consolidate the state budgetary process for UC, CSU and the community colleges. This would allow for greater coordination of programs at all levels and avoid administrative duplication. If downsizing is recommended, it should be done only after an analysis of student and state needs. Cutting expensive programs such as mechanical engineering and allowing the proliferation of large general education courses may gain an institution short-run dollars but won't truly serve the public interest.

Second, UC must seriously examine its commitment to educating undergraduates and streamline its graduate degrees. It has been fashionable for UC faculty to argue that they cannot do quality research with a heavier teaching load. But UC administrators would be hard-pressed to prove empirically that a heavier teaching load—as it was, say, twenty-five years ago—resulted in lower quality scholarship. State dollars that are used to subsidize faculty for research should be distributed on a competitive basis, as occurs for CSU faculty. In addition, this should be viewed as seed money to promote and support those faculty members who can bring external dollars into the system.

Re-examining the incentive system for faculty will inevitably impact the sacred tenure system. Although the historical merits of tenure should not be discounted, the importance of this system needs to be seriously reconsidered. Should faculty members, after six years of employment, be guaranteed lifetime employment without any significant review of teaching and research other than for merit increases?

Third, the term "downsizing" has become a popular euphemism for mindlessly cutting programs and departments. Perhaps we should shift away from autonomous campuses and look at the big picture of higher education in the state. This will require coordination across campuses and state systems. We need to begin to coordinate faculty, departments and campuses across the systems and begin to ask some questions that may at first seem blasphemous. Does UC really need four Ph.D. programs in sociology (in Berkeley, Los Angeles, Davis and Santa Barbara)?

Finally, we need to re-examine how university regents and trustees are appointed. Higher education should not depend on the benevolence of a governor's political appointment. We should push for either elected board members or a selection panel that will review qualified nominees who are representative of the users of the system. It's time to end old theologies in higher education and start anew. Do we have the vision?

Los Angeles Times, January 6, 1993

Pulling Back from the Future
Lower budgets and higher enrollments are delivering a one-two punch to state college students—and to California.

Due to a number of factors including the state's declining fiscal condition and increasing student population, particularly among Latino and Asian students, a re-examination of the state's educational system must be moved forward. We must plan now if we wish to guarantee a quality education for future students. A major element of this planning should include, in my opinion, improving the productivity, or cost-effectiveness, of each college or university in the state. Tax payers are increasingly demanding that we be held accountable for the manner in which their tax dollars are spent.
—*Jack Scott*

RECENTLY, I had the good fortune of participating on the President's Commission on White House Fellowships. The commission provides an opportunity for individuals early in their careers to work with Cabinet-level officials and members of the President's staff. I plowed through impressive resumes of many of our future leaders, from a planetary scientist who worked with the Voyager imaging team to a poet and scholar in federal Indian law. The candidates represented the diversity of the nation in education, sex, ethnicity, race and class. All shared a drive to succeed, an insatiable desire to continue their education in the public arena and a commitment to contribute for the public good.

More often than not, they identified key mentors in education who had triggered their dormant zeal to pursue stellar career paths. They confirmed the critical role that higher education plays in providing the future leaders of this nation the skills to promote a just and democratic society.

Educational opportunity has proved to be the mortar that binds a diverse population and propels it to greatness. It provides not only the common ground for a polity, but also the technical training required for maintaining a competitive economy. Since the 1960s, the Golden State's political leaders have recognized that our economic future is inextricably linked to providing high-quality, affordable and accessible higher education to our high school graduates. Many of the state's productivity gains were realized not from regulatory reform or tax breaks for entrepreneurs, but by providing the research and training of individuals for key sectors in the California economy.

California higher education will face an explosive demand of seven hundred thousand additional students in the next fifteen years. Many of these students will reflect the new faces of California's workforce, and this multicultural student population will require universities and colleges to develop innovative teaching strategies. At the same time, the state's higher-education system is facing a financial crisis. Given the projected growth of the state economy and the revenues needed to sustain our three-segment system—community colleges, CSU and the UC—it is not possible to meet the increased student demand. Although many university administrators have eloquently articulated this crisis in terms of limited state funds, shrinking tax base and explosive enrollment, they have not eloquently portrayed the human suffering of shortsighted cutbacks.

Students who will be entering the state's colleges this fall will no longer pay fees; rather, they will pay tuition with no clear upper boundary. In the last two years, UC undergraduate fees have more than doubled, from approximately $1,820 per year to $4,039 for 1993–94. CSU tuition has gone from $780 three years ago to $1,788 for 1993–94. And if Governor Wilson gets his way, fees at the community colleges will go from $10 to $30 a unit—$50 for students who have a bachelor's degree. Next year, students will compete for space in larger classes and will have to live with uncertainty about whether it will be possible to complete a bachelor's degree in four years. Students who planned their schedules to balance work with school will soon realize that course enrollment does not guarantee course access. And parents who saved $40,000 nest eggs for their children's education will soon realize that for the class of 1997 or 1998, this is merely a down payment.

Can we block the downward spiral of higher education? Should we also view this as an opportunity to reform a system in dire need of repair? These two questions are being addressed by the legislature and key education administrators throughout the state. Many of these policy leaders are suggesting innovative solutions to the financial crisis facing higher education. Unfortunately, the public has not been fully informed.

- •People have the right to know what percentage of their dollars is used for instruction, for research and for administrative support.
- •Given our prior commitment to equal access, legislators should match set-asides for student financial aid with any fee or tuition increase. Social equity is a sine qua non for public education and no qualified student should be discriminated against because of financial status.
- •Joint research ventures, collaborative teaching projects and combined doctoral programs should be considered between CSU and UC.
- •Faculty, administrators and the public must not forget that quality undergraduate education is the underpinning for all higher education. The quality of undergraduate teaching will determine the state's competitive edge in the twenty-first century. It also will provide our workforce with the skills to survive and contribute as leaders in an increasingly complex and diverse global society.

Los Angeles Times, June 2, 1993

Perspectives on UCLA's Ethnic Studies Decision Con Departmental Status Is Critical

UCLA is committed to Chicano studies, but the interdepartmental structure enriches the entire curriculum.

I was very impressed with your column in the Los Angeles Times *today.*

You conveyed compelling arguments that our scholars need to embrace.

If scholarship is not given priority over rhetoric then we not only tokenize

our scholars, but we risk having our centers swept out of existence in the

growing conservative political tide.

—*Jesus Mena*

FROM THEIR INCEPTION, many Chicano studies programs and departments were viewed as vehicles to foster a broadening of intellectual discourse that would include as subjects Latinos, blacks and Asians. That many faculty and administrators were threatened by such a paradigm, which would require interdisciplinary scholarship, is not surprising, given the general bias in higher education that emphasizes specialization and rewards clear disciplinary boundaries for teaching and scholarship. Contrary to popular misconceptions, ethnic studies departments do not balkanize students and faculty along racial and ethnic lines. They are often the only departments on campus that provide the needed comparative analysis of communities that can only enhance the critical-thinking skills of all students and provide greater understanding of the racial and ethnic tensions that permeate American society. On many campuses, they are the only safe space for students to question the status quo and to begin the intellectual odyssey that has become more challenging for today's students.

Although campus administrators have argued that department status is not necessary with joint appointments and borrowing of faculty from other departments, not many departments would agree that such an academic structure promotes high-quality research and curriculum. Department status is critical for ethnic studies programs, since the need to develop a cohesive, interdisciplinary unit for curriculum development, teaching and research requires budgetary autonomy to select faculty that will best meet those needs.

It is well known that borrowed faculty and joint appointments are risky for untenured faculty. The onerous requirements for junior faculty to publish in disciplinary trade journals and the pressure to meet home department teaching obligations result in Chicano studies programs receiving little if any benefits from faculty who are borrowed or who share appointments.

Often, those joint faculty who do commit research and teaching time in Chicano studies suffer the wrath of their colleagues, either during the tenure and promotion process or through exclusion of perks. There must be a critical mass of scholars committed to the development of a program, and these individuals must be evaluated and hired by their peers. This is virtually impossible in Chicano studies programs or departments that rely on affirmative-action hires in other disciplines. The assumption that a Chicano in social welfare or literature has expertise or interest in Chicano studies due to his or her having brown skin is as ludicrous as assuming that an Anglo faculty member in physics has expertise in colonial history. Visionary education requires us to go beyond traditional models, to expand our intellectual horizons and to take risks on diversity that initially challenge the status quo. This is beyond the politics of entitlement, but a recognition of legitimate areas of investigation.

Los Angeles Times, May 18, 1993

Perspective on Ethnic Studies: Activism Isn't Enough Anymore
Scholarship and intellectual rigor are required if programs are to move into the academic mainstream.

Really enjoyed your article in the Times *today, Dr. de la Torre, and I quite agree. I believe that access to academic positions based on political correctness, or the perception of being an insider only serves to emphasize conceptions of victimhood. It is surely the spirit of the academy to allow free discourse and dialogue across disciplines, and yet we fall short so often.*

—Philip V. Spradling

AS MY FIRST SEMESTER ENDS at the University of Arizona, I have just begun to understand the depth of the perils faced by directors of ethnic studies programs. Unlike more traditional departments, these programs emerged from the civil rights unrest of the 1960s and reflect, more often than not, the rhetoric of that era. It was a time when ethnic and racial authenticity were the criteria for entrance into these programs, and scholarly accomplishment meant little. Unfortunately, this legacy has created a fundamental contradiction as new scholars emerge with sterling credentials and academic legitimacy. People like Henry Louis Gates at Harvard, Ronald Takaki at UC Berkeley and Renato Rosaldo at Stanford are significant scholars involved in academic centers devoted to ethnic and racial issues. But at other such centers, many of those in charge chafe at the mention of scholarship having more weight than activist authenticity.

What may appear to be a minor difference of emphasis manifests in potential problems that threaten the academic success of ethnic studies programs. When I became director of the Mexican American Studies and Research Center here, the curriculum and lack of full-time faculty meant there was little structure or accountability to either the students or the administration. Last spring, an internal review of the center had recommended its elimination due to lack of productivity. My own review of student records found that more than 40 percent of the majors in this program could not pass the minimum writing requirements for the upper division, and these students were graduating without remediation or recommendations for writing intervention. It was clear that the center had failed to provide the basic skills in critical thinking and writing necessary for a successful application in a graduate program or on the job.

Mexican American studies is similar to other interdisciplinary studies, such as African American studies or programs in public health. But in a political sense, ethnic studies programs are very different, being products of civil unrest. Any changes in ethnic studies have political implications for the distribution of power within and outside the university. It is in this sense that any changes must be viewed not only as academic, but also as symbolic. And it is here that the academic credibility of ethnic studies becomes severely compromised.

Critics of ethnic studies programs are correct when they assert that curricula do not reflect the intellectual rigor of established disciplines. This is because of lack of expertise and scholarship in the area during the 1960s and into the 1970s. By the 1980s, however, emerging scholarship in racial and ethnic issues developed the foundation for a strong interdisciplinary field. By the 1990s, academic concerns over the issues of multiculturalism, diversity and race relations had created a dynamic dialogue across traditional disciplines and ethnic studies programs. This was captured symbolically when Harvard University established a highly visible African American studies program with Gates and other top scholars in the field.

It is not surprising that administrators across the country have begun to review their ethnic studies programs. Yet often, as here at the University of Arizona, the path to transform a program from mediocrity to excellence requires challenging the status quo of political brokers from the past so that the program could meet the demands of an elite institution. One need only reflect on the divisive struggle over Rodolfo Acuña's fight for a tenured position at UC Santa Barbara to recognize the high stakes involved.

If ethnic studies is to achieve credibility in academia as well as in society, leaders must shift away from the rhetoric of the 1960s to the substantive merit of the scholarship. Minorities are not victims of the system but masters of their own destiny. We must develop a scholarship and understanding of the issues that face minority populations so that we can provide students and faculty with requisite skills to work together.

The battle for the soul of ethnic studies is between those who want to maintain isolation, cultural nationalism and the litmus test of authenticity based on political values and others who view diversity of opinion, diversity of scholars and academic rigor as keys to success. In the context of many ethnic studies programs, this latter point of view is seen as threatening, because it implies that "outsiders" may gain entry to the insiders' politically gained spots.

Yet if ethnic studies programs do not open their intellectual doors, the promise of intellectual equality becomes merely an illusion in the academy and we will continue to tokenize our scholars. Moreover, we will push away the critical dialogue that has been necessary in shaping every new discipline.

Los Angeles Times, December 12, 1996

I Think, Therefore I Am
Relying on talk radio to validate our feelings has become an easy way to avoid intellectual discussion and debate.

I read with interest your editorial, "Rethinking Higher Education." I applaud you for raising such sharp, thoughtful, and urgent questions about the productiveness of our system of public higher education. . . . I encourage you to continue to seek audiences for your ideas. Perhaps your editorial . . . could serve to help advance a careful and intelligent scrutiny of our state's delivery of education.

—Jack Scott

WHEN THE NEW CONGRESSIONAL FRESHMAN CLASS opted to forgo orientation at Harvard's Kennedy School of Government, many interpreted it as a shift away from the liberal Northeast academic climate to a more conservative place, which would reaffirm the ideology of the Republicans' new "contract with America." But this, combined with Newt Gingrich's support for cutting funding for public broadcasting, is the unsettling message that intellectuals, particularly academics, are no longer necessary in the public discourse of politics.

There is little doubt that underlying this is the view that academics are a privileged elite who have no understanding of the daily battles of survival for the middle class. The growing demonization of intellectuals in American society speaks to a real danger that threatens governance based on reason and civil discourse.

This is not to suggest that academics do not share responsibility for their own growing isolation from the general public. Clearly, the trend toward greater specialization in research and publication in arcane journals creates an insular life. And leaders in higher education have not been effective in communicating that university faculty are relevant to everyday life. In general, those in higher education have been unsuccessful in moving forward the cause for educated reason over emotional response in the debates for social change. Moreover, as academics become increasingly marginalized from mainstream society, their fundamental status as the nation's educators becomes suspect.

There is no doubt that the media have played a role in fueling the anti-intellectualism that permeates political debate. Rush Limbaugh's success is linked not only to his ability to validate the visceral emotions of the middle class, but also to the networks' unwillingness to risk profit levels for programs that require greater literacy from the general public. In many ways, the new opiate for most Americans has become the soothing drone of simple-minded chatter that minimizes "book learning" and reaffirms personal beliefs. This new community of media "intellectuals" who enter our homes and our lives has replaced the front-porch discussions of years past.

Tabloid journalists and talk-show hosts pander to our deepest insecurities, further distancing us from more intellectual pursuits. But the cost of such distancing could be the success of our market system. An electorate that is unwilling to tax itself mentally and enter into heated political discussions based on literacy and knowledge does not bode well for America's future in the world order.

Liberals and conservatives must not ignore the significance of literacy in informed decision-making. This includes a thorough understanding of an opponent's point of view. Both reciprocity and tolerance are necessary for the best solution to evolve. Though emotional responses about political issues may develop, they should not dehumanize an opponent. Meaningful debate about social policy always includes judgments, but reason should triumph.

University classrooms are almost the only places left where there are civil discussions of complex issues. And even there, emotions must be controlled to allow for competing interests to examine social issues. Most college students realize that a requirement for participation in a discussion is knowledge of the topic. As students thirst for additional knowledge, the notion of absolute truth comes into question. Relative truth and global complexity emerge as unsettling catalysts.

This painful academic process, which pushes the boundaries of our intellects and forces us to understand, not vilify, our opponents, is a model that must re-emerge in the public arena. Respecting differences and developing consensus are basic skills in most classrooms, but are lacking in today's political arena, where middle-class feelings have become of greater concern. This focus on emotions rather than reason has further fueled anti-intellectualism.

Middle-class people are the new victims in American society, but the victimization is not from big government or higher taxes, but from their own intellectual malaise. As the middle class points fingers at the poor, at big government, at immigrants, it must begin pointing at itself and taking responsibility for an unwillingness to think.

Los Angeles Times, January 4, 1995

Reflections on Higher Education Today

Key themes in the 1990s that influenced the debates surrounding higher education in California included the following: the declining funding and political support for public higher education; reforming higher education and the tenure system; the need for greater representation of Latino faculty in universities; increasing interest in the development and assessment of ethnic studies programs; and public demonization of the academy and intellectuals.

The debate over funding public higher education during the 1990s was linked to the precarious California economy as well as to a public perception that Californians had a right to a highly subsidized, low-cost college education system. This perception was an outgrowth of Clark Kerr's vision of an elaborate community college, a CSU system, and an elite UC system, which would provide open access to higher education for all Californians in the post–World War II era. Unfortunately, the rapid growth of the 1960s and 1970s began to taper during the late 1970s, as the baby boom generation started to graduate from this highly subsidized system. As the demographic profile of a largely white college student population shifted to a more diverse student body, political interest in higher education began to decline. The demographic shift, combined with the state's greater economic uncertainty, decreased the public's concern over adequate funding for higher education. In addition, sensationalized issues such as crime, quality of life and immigration shifted support away from maintaining equal access and quality of education, particularly for Latinos and other minority groups.

The 1990s were marked by rapid growth in the number of students served by the public higher education system, and at the same time, waning support for the original mission of universal access for all Californians. As cost increased, access to the best public universities and colleges decreased for minorities. This created enormous inter-racial/ethnic conflict, because few spots were available in the most competitive institutions like UCLA and UC Berkeley. This also instigated the process of reviewing admissions criteria that included race and ethnicity as variables in the admission process by the UC regents. Ward Connerly, an African American regent within the UC system, played a pivotal role in this debate as he represented the constituency opposed to the use of affirmative action in higher education admissions policies.

The issues of limited resources and lack of higher educational access for minority populations continue to fester. In many respects, the problems have been exacerbated by the failure of public schools to adequately prepare minority students for college. We now face an even greater dilemma, because the reversal of affirmative action in higher education has decreased the pool of both minority faculty and students in elite institutions. California's anti-affirmative action efforts have negatively affected the enrollment status of Latinos in graduate and professional schools: they have the lowest enrollment of minority groups other than American Indians. In 1996, Latinos represented a mere 4 percent of all graduate students in the nation's universities. In 1995, Latinos represented only 2 percent of all full-time faculty and teaching positions in the United States.[1] California is one of the major states producing Latino professionals and Ph.D.'s through its vast public university system. Thus, any decrease in graduate minority education in California has a direct impact on the pool of Latino minority scholars nationwide.

Other important themes of the 1990s that still ring true today are the need to reform higher education with respect to tenure and greater faculty responsiveness to the community. Tenure, theoretically, exists to protect academic freedom, an important and noble concept rooted in an earlier time when university faculty members were vulnerable to the political whims of power brokers in government and business. Today, as it was in the 1990s, the issue of protecting academic freedom appears to be less important than protecting job security for faculty. In most institutions of higher education, there are ample mechanisms to address issues impinging on academic freedom in the classroom and in research. In light of the significant internal university processes as well as the external civil processes to address academic freedom, it becomes more difficult for institutions and faculty to defend tenure. More rigorous post-tenure review processes are becoming increasingly common across the country as a way to address poor teaching and research. The effect of such reviews is changing the notion of lifelong tenure in an institution. Moreover, given the change in the career cycle of individuals and broader acceptance of higher job turnover for professional reasons, tenure itself may no longer be the main factor in keeping the best faculty on university campuses.

Latino faculty entering this new post-tenure climate fall within two camps with respect to the tenure debate. The first camp views the post-tenure debate as a direct attack on their newfound mobility and job security within predominantly white institutions of higher education. That is, now that there is a small but critical mass of Latino scholars in the academy, the opportunity for tenure and intellectual security is eliminated for them. The ultimate conclusion from this point of view is that the post-tenure debates reflect a continuation of the institutional racism that excludes Latinos from higher education.

The other point of view reflects a more pragmatic perspective on the global changes affecting higher education. That is, higher education and the process of retention and tenure must change to serve a more mobile, technologically dependent, and diverse society. Tenure and the tenure process within the academy have not served the Latino community well. As few Latino faculty are tenured, the largely white, male professorate dominate the political discourse of the academy. Given this reality, Latino faculty are at a distinct disadvantage, and although this group may value the notion of academic freedom that tenure represents, they have not been the direct beneficiaries of this entitlement. One need only look at the percentage of Latino faculty in institutions of higher education to understand the need for continued aggressive affirmative action efforts as a mechanism to increase the number of graduate students, faculty and administrators.

The dearth of Latino faculty in tenure track positions has resulted in a crisis in mentorship and leadership for Latino students within the academy. Latino faculty continue to be tokenized, isolated within individual departments, or stigmatized if they focus their research within their own ethnic group. Although there are ethnic studies programs on many campuses, these programs are also marginalized in the academy by either the continued perception of their inferior scholarly quality or by lack of financial and administrative support. Having participated in ethnic studies program reviews at a national level, I have heard several recurring complaints from ethnic studies faculty. These include a general sense of isolation from the broader university community, a real sense of overt deprivation of resources, a lack of recognition of their contributions to the university's intellectual environment, and an underlying frustration resulting from the inherent bias of the majority professorate against programs that focus their academic research on minority populations. This has created a siege mentality in many of these programs, as they are justifiably concerned not only with their survival, but also with the continued decline of support by their respective university administrations.

There is no doubt that ethnic studies programs play a critical role in the intellectual climate of colleges and universities. However, given the changing resource base in higher education and greater need for accountability, traditional ethnic studies models may need to change. As indicated in my editorial "Activism Is Not Enough," the political and economic climate as well as the mix of student ethnic identity have shifted. For example, the cry for cultural nationalism that was so powerful in the 1960s and early 1970s no longer has the same impact on a Latino student's identity. This becomes more apparent as regional differences within Latino groups become more visible. Having taught Latino students in three states—Colorado, California, and Arizona—I have observed within the last eighteen years the reluctance of Mexican-origin students to identify themselves as Chicano. This is particularly true in the border region of Arizona, where students from Nogales, most of whom are of Mexican origin, largely define themselves as Mexican. This is not a negation of political consciousness but a reflection of Arizona's proximity to Mexico, where many students have deep familial and social ties that define their identity.[2] In states like Colorado, which have a smaller immigrant population than California and are not on the border, there appears to be a wider range of identity as compared to Arizona. In California, perceptions of identity are different in the north and the south. For the larger immigrant population in southern California, identity is rooted in the home country of the Latino immigrant. In northern California, within the Latino ethnic enclaves, there appears to be a more fluid and open definition of identity, ranging from Latino/a, to Chicano/a, to more specific labels that mirror multiple ethnic, racial, and gender identities.

Cultural nationalism as a unifying force for young people in the twenty-first century continues to be effective in the penal system. For example, Mexican/Chicano and other Latino gangs have used it to define their turf and power within the oppressive environment of the U.S. prison system. As articulated by one former inmate who served time at Pelican Bay State Prison, the Chicano identity represents a common unifier among inmates of Mexican descent and is reinforced by the prison system itself:

I have been in this "hole" now ever since the prison first opened its serpent like jaw in December 1989; transferred here from

another California prison for my alleged gang ties, a common label placed on those of latin extraction by the California Department of Corrections. You see, ironically 95 percent of the inmates in this Security Housing Unit are Chicanos, and of course allegedly affiliated to one gang or other according to the C.D.C.,—imagin that! . . . I for one, am an example of one of those you described in your column. A Chicano, whose youthful life was wasted away in warehouses such as the one I now find my self in; because of my own, as well as societies ignorance.
—Hector Gallegos

Today, however, because young Latinos do not readily perceive discrimination as it is linked to their ethnicity, the importance of cultural nationalism is mitigated in many academic environments. Where does this leave ethnic studies programs in the twenty-first century? Clearly, they have not been supported at the level necessary for academic success, yet bemoaning the lack of resources will not change the situation. Although the new generation of ethnic studies scholars, including Chicano and Chicana faculty, are not rooted in the rhetoric of the 1970s, it is important to recognize the historical significance of the Chicano Movement in formulating present-day Chicana and Chicano studies programs. With the development of multicultural studies programs and greater interest in promoting a pan-ethnic identity among all Latino groups, ethnic studies programs that focus solely on one ethnic group are waning. Thus, the philosophy and rhetoric of previous Chicana and Chicano studies programs will guide fewer ethnic studies scholars in their intellectual pursuits. Because of shifting interests, the litmus test of ethnic identity and political perspective no longer dominates many academic circles of Chicana and Chicano studies. Yet, the shift to embrace pan-ethnicity may not be in the best interest of programs geared to improving the daily lives of Latinos through academic research. We still need ethnic-specific programs to address the myriad of problems of our respective Latino communities. Moreover, the different Latino subgroups require attention to their community-specific concerns. In essence, for Chicano/Latino studies programs to regain momentum and support from their respective communities, they must provide practical solutions to historical problems.

Notes

1. "The Chronicle 1999–2000 Almanac," *Chronicle of Higher Education,* accessed at http://chronicle.com/weekly/almanac/1999/facts/6folks.htm, July 6, 2000.

2. For more information on ethnic identity in the border region see Oscar J. Martínez, *Border People: Life and Society in the U.S.-Mexico Borderlands* (Tucson: University of Arizona Press, 1994).

CHAPTER 4

AFFIRMATIVE
ACTION

For Women, for Minorities, for Us All,
Preserve Affirmative Action

**Society as a whole benefits when all its members have access to
decent education and opportunities.**

*The tone of your column makes you sound like someone to whom I can
pose thoughts and questions you might address in future columns. From
my perspective, the articles, columns, and letters-to-the-editor I've seen
over the decades on the Hispanic issues in general have been very uninfor-
mative and frustrating in trying to understand "the other side." While I
don't presume to speak for the entire European-origin population of the
United States, I am sure my perceptions are not unique.*

—Thomas Erskine

I GRADUATED FROM UC BERKELEY and scored relatively well on
my Graduate Record Exam. Because of finances—I could live at
home—I had only one choice for graduate school, my alma mater.
I planned to finance my education as a research assistant for a fac-

ulty member in my department. But though I had a graduate minority fellowship that provided for my tuition, I was denied a research assistantship. After a year of haggling with the Byzantine university bureaucracy to understand why, I filed a complaint with the Equal Employment Opportunity Commission (EEOC). I never received my assistantship, but the EEOC investigation forced the department to recognize that opening their doors would require some adjustments.

Affirmative action programs have never been painless in higher education. But for women and underrepresented groups, affirmative action programs have widened opportunities in education. In my case, these programs not only opened the doors for my present career, but also exposed me to the endemic biases in academia with regard to women and people of color. In the last twenty-five years, we have seen a plethora of affirmative action programs arise in the private and the public sectors. Despite the current rhetoric, affirmative action is hardly a radical departure from a merit-based system. Rather, these programs reflect a rational and incremental approach to remedying past discrimination as well as ensuring equal opportunity. In the context of social policies that influence market outcomes, affirmative action is far less restrictive than our national labor laws, which place considerable constraints on individual rights and markets.

But a mythology has developed around affirmative action that tells of unqualified minorities and women entering jobs and universities to the detriment of qualified white males. In these stories, quotas abound and qualified minority applicants suffer due to their perceived inferior status as affirmative action entrants. But the evidence is quite different. For example, since the Supreme Court's *Bakke* decision in 1978, quotas or set-asides have been illegal, though the decision upheld the notion that race could be viewed as a "plus" factor to foster student body diversity. The more recent (1995) *Adarand* decision, which focused on federal contracts, strengthened the notion that affirmative action programs must be able to withstand strict scrutiny based on evidence of discrimination.

In higher education, affirmative action has played a critical role in increasing participation by women and other under-represented groups. A recent study by the American Council of Education found that:

- In 1994, 44 percent of all college students were women and 46 percent of doctorates awarded to U.S. citizens went to women, up from 25 percent two decades earlier.
- From 1984 to 1994, minority enrollment in the nation's colleges and universities increased by 63 percent.
- Between 1985 and 1993, bachelor's degrees were up 36 percent among African Americans, 34 percent among American Indians, 75 percent among Latinos and nearly 103 percent among Asian Americans.

Opponents of affirmative action often ignore the real value added to society when diverse U.S. constituents are better educated. On the other hand, supporters of affirmative action must also be reminded that such programs are effective only on the margin and will never redistribute wealth or opportunity. At best, these programs recognize our painful legacy of racism and sexism by infusing the notion of individual merit with historical and present reality.

As the political battle over the California Civil Rights Initiative (CCRI) heats up during the next few months, we will witness the increased demonization of affirmative action programs as we have with welfare, Medicare and immigration. Most politicians and people in the media know that there is much to be gained by a reasoned debate over affirmative action. But as we all sink into visceral responses and populist rhetoric, we may lose more than affirmative action next November. We may lose control over our own destiny.

Los Angeles Times, April 10, 1996

Diversity, Not Quotas, for Colleges

Sharing of intellectual space both educates and empowers students. But campuses should beware of bureaucratic tokenism.

Whether the United States is a salad bowl or a melting pot, we honor the rights of individuals. . . . This, however, is a different issue from the one which seeks to create a common society out of a myriad of persons, cultures, languages, and backgrounds. This is a difficult task at best. Without a common purpose it is impossible.

—Dave Walters

CAMPUS DIVERSITY is now a measure of a university's success. But unlike affirmative action programs that have polarized faculty both on the left and on the right by their narrow, bureaucratic intrusions on faculty selection, there has yet to be a standardized policy developed for achieving campus diversity. Campuses most engaged in the diversity debate are those that have seen the most change in their undergraduate student population in the last five years. Faculty discussions on diversity do not mirror the affirmative action agenda, because diversity is not defined solely by race, sex or ethnicity but includes sexual preference, age, income and educational background.

For elite institutions such as Harvard or Yale, discussions of diversity have little immediate relevance due to selection processes that ensure a relatively homogeneous student population—that is, Harvard may have a racial and ethnic mix, but from a relatively homogeneous class background.

On the other hand, public institutions such as the California State University (CSU) system draw from public high schools. Demographic shifts in enrollment and differences in income levels of students are forcing CSU faculty to address the issue of diversity to increase their own teaching effectiveness. This is based on neither moral nor political grounds, but rather on pragmatism, to ensure that we teachers can meet our students' needs.

Diversity in higher education forces faculty and administrators to accept new power relationships. In the past, curricula were rigidly defined by faculty experts, but diversity requires breaking traditional disciplinary boundaries and acknowledging that curricula must be expanded to train our students in applied skills and critical thinking. Faculty must become more creative to retain undergraduate students and maintain their quality of instruction.

The incentive to hire diverse faculty does not stem from government mandates and quotas, nor should advocates of diversity allow affirmative action bureaucrats to reduce the debate to tokenism and color-coding applicants. Rather, the discussion should be rooted in the comparative advantage that departments will have in hiring educators who are better equipped in the method as well as the content of teaching. We expand the base of knowledge that will prepare students to compete in the global market by including in their portfolio of knowledge an understanding of diverse cultures, history and languages.

Those opposed to diversity in education fear the loss of quality and continued balkanization of our student population, and that group rights will take precedence over individual rights. Yet a major goal of such curricula is to provide a platform for acknowledging individual differences, particularly those within groups. From this knowledge, students should begin to recognize a common ground where alliances can form.

As an economist who recently began teaching in ethnic studies, I value the opportunity of using contemporary Chicano scholarship to teach students who would normally view economics as irrelevant to their lives. Adam Smith's *Wealth of Nations* shares the bookshelf with Chicana scholars. By whetting students' intellectual appetite with relevant literature, I open the path for acceptance of alternative views and disciplines. This sharing of intellectual space is not a pedagogy of entitlement; rather, it is a pedagogy of empowerment.

That few faculty on college campuses have opportunities for cross-disciplinary teaching is unfortunate. Yet we who are on increasingly diverse campuses know that curriculum change is inevitable. Shifting power relationships within departments and colleges will result in acrimonious academic struggles not only in the

CSU system, but also at the University of California (UC), where doctoral education will require greater public scrutiny to ensure that graduate-student training meets the hiring needs of state universities.

Diversity in our student population has forced us to challenge ourselves and our disciplines to regain student trust and public confidence. Though no college has resolved the issue of diversity in the intellectual playing field, we know that if it is to be effective, it must go beyond political correctness, tokenism and bureaucratic manipulation of faculty and curricula.

Los Angeles Times, Commentary, March 19, 1994

Diversifying Classrooms Is the Key to Improving the Economy

In the political arena, phrases like "sensitive to the needs of Hispanics" often appear. Yet these "needs" are never specified. What do "the Hispanics" need from the various levels of government that's different from the rest of us?

—Thomas Erskine

TODAY, affirmative action programs in universities and colleges are at a crossroads. Across the nation public institutions of higher education are subject to a barrage of criticism from the electorate and public governing boards that view affirmative action as "reverse discrimination." In California, an anti-affirmative action initiative on the November ballot, the California Civil Rights Initiative (CCRI), spearheaded by African American UC regent Ward Connerly, has polarized the state across race, ethnic and gender lines. In Texas, the recent *Hopwood* decision against the University of Texas law school, further threatens the viability of affirmative action programs in public institutions of higher education. Yet, despite the current hullabaloo over affirmative action, it still remains the most effective mechanism of meeting the challenge of integrating a large segment of society into the American mainstream. Indeed, these types of programs reflect a commitment to diversity shared by several elite institutions of higher education since the mid-nineteenth century.

The recent Harvard University President's Report highlights the importance of diversity as an explicit goal for one of Harvard's most important presidents, Charles Elliot. For Elliot, president of Harvard between 1869 and 1909, heterogeneity within the student population was a necessary ingredient for a vibrant education. As stated in the recent President's Report, Elliot wanted "a university of broad democratic resort . . . children of the rich and poor, the educated and uneducated."[1] Although one of Elliot's key goals in setting this agenda was to foster greater religious tolerance within the United States, the broader impact was to end the criteria for admission to elite institutions beyond the established meritocratic system of the time. Since then leaders in elite institutions of higher education have followed Elliot's challenge, viewing admission criteria to the university as not subject to the public demands of the present, but subject to the needs of creating a more democratic future.

It is in this spirit that we have seen the motivation and success of contemporary affirmative action programs in higher education. There is no doubt that affirmative action has played a central role in diversifying our faculty and our students. Since the 1970s, the numerical gains in college admissions and postgraduate education have been strongly linked to the aggressive development and refinement of affirmative action programs. For example, in the last two decades targeted efforts to increase the representation of women in higher education has increased the number of female college students and doctorates awarded to women by 25 percent. In the last ten years, minority enrollment in colleges and universities has increased by 63 percent.

Many of the gains in higher education are translated into better jobs and wages for women and minorities. From the early 1900s until the mid-1970s, the female-to-male wage ratio was 60 percent. According to one federal study, by 1993 the wage gap was reduced by half. Similarly, when we examine the income gains made by minority groups during the last twenty years, both anti-discrimination legislation as well as affirmative action programs played key roles in breaking down educational barriers that allowed for subsequent employment gains for African Americans, Latinos and other minority groups.

By both providing diversity to college campuses as well as improving the market skills of underserved populations, affirmative action programs have met the challenge of weaving disparate groups onto a platform where dialogue can begin and a stronger democracy can emerge. By bringing diversity into the classroom, these programs move forward Charles Elliot's vision of a university where: "This collision of views is wholesome and profitable; it promotes thought on great themes, converts passion into resolution, cultivates forbearance and mutual respect and teaches . . . candor, moral courage and independence of thought on whatever side these noble qualities may be displaced."[2]

Minorities in Business, Fall/Winter 1996

Executive Briefing: Affirmative Action

FOR MANY HISPANIC small businesses, affirmative action goes beyond the university classroom to the dollars and cents of federal contracts. A recent White House report on affirmative action spells out why Hispanic businesses should be concerned with the affirmative action debate as it affects their strategies to integrate and compete in a bias-free market. According to this White House study, there are several key issues important to socially disadvantaged groups. At the very top of the list, Hispanic businesses should keep an eye on programs such as the Small Business Administration's Section 8(a).

Federal initiatives like Section 8(a) seek to enhance participation in procurement by minority- and women-owned firms. These programs evolved to integrate these small companies into the mainstream business community. Several of these programs were tested successfully in the Supreme Court in the 1970s, when the history of clear discrimination against minorities was visible in business practices that overtly excluded minorities from traditional business networks. These networks were deemed critical to submitting successful bids for federal contracts. The federal government also recognized that discrimination in business practices was not the only deterrent to successful minority business bids for federal contracts. Minority firms were plagued with problems such as limited access to finances as well as lack of familiarity with the federal bidding process, which further hindered minority participation.

The Supreme Court's *Adarand v. Peña* decision has narrowed the criteria for sheltered federal programs, but it has not eliminated the need for such programs. *Adarand* strengthened the requirement of strict scrutiny for programs that address present—not past—effects of racial discrimination. Despite anecdotal commentary that "quotas" abound in federal contracting, there is little in the current data or legal precedent that would suggest they exist. Indeed, minority procurement programs have barely scratched the surface in integrating the federal prime contract market, where recent estimates indicate that minority businesses receive about 3 percent of the more than $200 billion prime contract budget.

As Hispanics increase their overall percentage in the general population, they have yet to reach parity in business ownership. U.S. Hispanics own about 5 percent of all U.S. businesses; these companies garner 2.3 percent of all receipts. Many Hispanic firms that are successful today can trace their success to sheltered federal sole-source contracts under 8(a) programs. These programs allowed small, disadvantaged businesses the opportunity to obtain contracts without open competition. The White House report states that one in five of the one hundred largest Latino-owned businesses participated in 8(a) programs in 1994. The participation of African-American firms was even higher, with almost one-third of the top one hundred black-owned firms participating in these programs during this same time period.

Benefits from these sheltered programs reach beyond the actual contract work; preliminary evidence gathered by the Small Business Administration (SBA) indicates that graduate companies tend to stay in business longer than non-participants. In addition, given the location of many of these minority-owned businesses in economically depressed areas, 8(a) programs have the added benefit of providing private-sector jobs in underserved areas. Thus, they have the unique potential of jump-starting depressed communities by circulating money where it is most needed.

Although much of the debate on sheltered competition and "set-asides" has targeted minority entrepreneurs, it is important to note that the federal government has goals to integrate all small businesses into the lucrative federal procurement market. The SBA has established national goals based on federal law to increase all small business federal procurement participation by 20 percent.

Despite the current brouhaha over affirmative action, the current numbers pale compared to the goals needed to integrate groups into the federal contract mainstream. More than 90 percent of procurement remains in the hands of non-minority firms. Thus federal economic largess remains under the control of the majority population. Even large participants in this market recognize that without 8(a) programs, the prospects of significant participation in government procurement would regress back to the time when the courts, not the contractors, were busy rebuilding the playing field.

Hispanic Business Magazine, September 1996

New Frontiers for Diversity: The Death Knell of Affirmative Action

The affirmative action issue caused enormous political turmoil at the end of the twentieth century, and continues to do so now. A policy long championed by the Democratic Party, it has had many internal and external detractors. I have consistently felt compelled to support affirmative action. This is based on my personal experience as a product of these programs as well as an observer of higher education, where the current increase of women and minority faculty and students on college campuses can be attributed to affirmative action policies of the 1970s and 1980s. The following table illustrates the racial composition of all full-time faculty in universities nationwide as of 1995. As the table indicates, women have approximately 35 percent of all full-time faculty positions, with Hispanic women composing less than 1 percent. While minorities represent almost 13 percent of the total number of full-time faculty positions in the country, Hispanics represent only 2 percent.[3]

Table. Full-Time Faculty in U.S. Universities in 1995

	Total	American Indian	Asian	Black	Hispanic	White	Non-resident alien	Race Unknown
All	550,822	2,156	27,572	26,835	12,942	468,518	10,853	1,946
Men	360,150	1,262	20,285	13,847	7,864	307,498	8,161	1,233
Women	190,672	894	7,287	12,988	5,078	161,020	2,692	713

Source: The Chronicle of Higher Education 1999–2000 Almanac.

According to one senior Latina scholar,

In my experience, a Latina presence on a search committee can make a difference in terms of how fairly a Latina applicant is evaluated. . . . From my perspective, Latinas are evaluated in one of three ways: they are either viewed as "too nice" to make the tough administrative decisions or conversely "too aggressive" or "too whiney" to be an effective administrator. . . . while EuroAmerican [*sic*] men are rarely accused of lobbying for "their man" in a search situation, I've found that if a Latina seems too much of an "advocate" for "her candidate," her influence on the committee dwindles. . . . It takes courage for a woman of color to apply for these positions and to endure the gauntlet of the on-campus interview.

In light of the tremendous barriers facing women of color in hiring and promotion decisions in the academy, one would expect greater interest in retaining some form of affirmative action programs. However, *Hopwood,* a Fifth Circuit Court of Appeals case, challenged the use of aggressive affirmative action programs in higher education and has undermined university-based affirmative action programs as a means of increasing the enrollment of minority students in graduate and professional programs. *Hopwood* prohibited public higher educational institutions in Texas, Louisiana and Mississippi from using a prospective student's racial or ethnic background in recruitment, admission or retention activities, including scholarship programs that specifically target minorities for admission.[4] Moreover, affirmative action efforts continue to be challenged, as evidenced by the 1997 case of *Grutter v. The Regents of the University of Michigan,* in which a white woman filed a lawsuit alleging unlawful preference for minorities in the university's law school admissions.[5] These challenges, combined with state initiatives to outlaw affirmative action in public agencies, such as Proposition 209 in California and Proposition 200 in Washington state, have had a chilling effect on minority enrollment in colleges across the country. For example, the most egregious impact of *Hopwood* was seen in medical education, where the overall number of minority medical school applicants dropped 8.4 percent in 1997. Due to the effect of the *Hopwood* decision, minority students were discouraged from applying to professional schools because of the fear that they would not be given due consideration in the application process. In Texas, had the state not passed its 10 percent rule after the *Hopwood* case, minority admission into its most prestigious public institution, University of Texas, Austin, would have been virtually eliminated. The 10 percent rule stipulates that the top 10 percent of each graduating high school in the state will be automatically admitted to the University of Texas, Austin, thus assuring minority enrollment.

The insidious effect of anti–affirmative action proponents on college campuses has resulted in complacency with respect to promoting diversity. It is perfectly acceptable these days to allow state-supported universities to have low rates of minority graduate student enrollment. Undergraduate programs like sociology, political science, psychology, and history that should attract minority applicants into their graduate programs based on the pool of undergraduate majors have virtually no minority doctoral students and produce few minority Ph.D.'s. For example, my own institution, the University of Arizona, awarded relatively few Ph.D.'s to Hispanics in the College of Social and Behavioral Sciences between

1991 and 1999. Of those Hispanic students who did receive Ph.D.'s, eight were in anthropology, one in geography, two in history, two in linguistics, one in philosophy, two in political science, five in psychology, and two in sociology. The total number of Ph.D.'s for the same period in this college was 505, meaning that less than one percent of all Ph.D.'s were awarded to Hispanic students. These shocking figures attest not only to the gross underrepresentation of Hispanic students at the doctoral level, but also to the blatant disregard of this issue by the white professoriate. Most of the faculty in these programs are older white men, who choose to mentor individuals with similar interests and backgrounds. The net impact of this preference is minority students being ignored or avoided by faculty and the tacit approval of institutional racism within the faculty ranks, thereby leaving minority students and junior faculty outside of the academic mentoring loop. With no visible leadership with respect to graduate student diversity from deans, department chairs and presidents, there is little hope that affirmative action can be replaced by the good will of university faculty.

Even with affirmative action, proponents of diversity in higher education were always caught in the politics of hiring. Most university administrators were concerned with meeting affirmative action rules that were consistent with federal Equal Employment Opportunity Commission (EEOC) policies. That is, their priority was not diversity in hiring, but ensuring compliance with federal guidelines. Federal rules do not change hiring practices in universities unless the organizational culture and faculty incentives change to reward diversity in hiring, retention and promoting of minority faculty and administrators.

The overall concern with meeting bureaucratic standards to avoid litigation or reprimand, as opposed to aggressive efforts to enhance diversity within individual departments and the highest levels of leadership, has thus created a major crisis with respect to meeting diversity goals in the academy. Affirmative action opponents falsely argue that using race, ethnicity and gender as a criteria in admission results in a direct loss of income and resources for white applicants. However, this program only operates on the margin, not as a direct substitute for standard hiring and/or admissions criteria. If the program is correctly implemented, race, ethnicity and gender are additional considerations once the standards have been met. Unqualified individuals are not admitted or hired under affirmative action programs. This marginal change had a positive impact on professional programs, particularly medical and law schools. In addition, in those universities that used "target of opportunity" hiring strategies to increase the number of minority faculty, these programs made inroads into traditionally white male–dominated disciplines by adding one to two faculty members in some departments.

In light of the shift away from affirmative action, what alternatives exist for higher education? Perhaps the best example of an alternative for promoting diversity and increasing the pool of minority students in public universities is the previously discussed 10 percent admissions rule in the state of Texas. Beyond the 10 percent rule, the University of Texas restructured its merit-based recruitment and scholarship programs that specifically targeted underrepresented minority students. The university was forced to abolish bona fide affirmative action programs and shift to a method based on students' socioeconomic backgrounds and financial needs as a means of increasing and maintaining diversity.[6] While this strategy has resulted in a greater number of undergraduate minority students at the University of Texas, it has not been as effective in increasing the number of minority graduate and professional students, because it focuses on undergraduate admission. Nonetheless, policies like the 10 percent rule and needs-based programs that focus on non–race specific criteria to enhance enrollment of economically disadvantaged students from different ethnic backgrounds will most likely continue as the preferred admissions strategy at public institutions.

The dilemma of minority student admissions in graduate and professional schools, however, still remains an urgent problem for both public and private institutions. This problem can only be resolved if college admissions committees begin to recognize a broader range of criteria when considering minority applicants. For example, in the admissions process for both law school and medical school, community service, work experience and the applicant's professional statements should be scrutinized with equal consideration as standardized test scores and grades. By including these other factors, we will be better able to consider diversity criteria in admissions of not only minority students but also nontraditional white applicants, such as re-entry older students, who show promise in their prospective fields. Currently, several graduate and professional programs successfully use this strategy in their admissions process without adverse effects to their programs.

Finally, an important strategy that will continue throughout the next few years will be more aggressive development of K–12 intervention and outreach programs that encourage young minority students to aspire to higher education and advanced degrees. Such programs include the Business Leadership Program (LEAD), the Heath Career Opportunity Program (HCOP), and the Minority Introduction to Engineering, Entrepreneurship, and Science (MITE). These national efforts target minority and economically disadvantaged youth for opportunities in business, health and engineering during their critical high school years. To build on the gains made in the past twenty years in making higher education more equitable and open, a comprehensive strategy should be employed that includes early outreach, open admissions based on a standard rule such as the Texas 10 percent rule, and the consideration of a broader base of information in assessing graduate school applicants. Such plans may provide viable alternatives to dead and wounded affirmative action programs. In addition, a recent decision by University of California Regents to reverse its previous ban on affirmative action in the UC system may also prove to increase underrepresented minority enrollment in higher education institutions such as UC Berkeley and UCLA.

Notes

1. *The President's Report 1993–1995: Diversity and Learning*, Harvard University.

2. Ibid.

3. The following information was obtained from the "The Chronicle 1999–2000 Almanac," *Chronicle of Higher Education*, accessed at http://chronicle.com/weekly/almanac/1999/facts/6folks.htm, July 6, 2000.

4. In *Hopwood, et al. vs. State of Texas, et al.*, four students filed suit after they were denied admittance to the University of Texas law school in 1992. The

lawsuit alleged that the four students were denied admission because of their race and sought changes in the school's admission policy as well as punitive damages. Albert Kauffman, "The Hopwood Case—What It Says, What It Doesn't Say, the Future of the Case and 'the Rest of the Story'," *IRDA Newsletter,* accessed at http://www.idra.org/Newslttr/1996/Aug/Albert.htm, April 27, 2001.

5. On March 27, 2001, a federal district court issued its ruling in *Grutter v. The Regents of the University of Michigan.* The court ruled that the University's admissions policy, which used race as a factor in considering applicants for admission, was unconstitutional. The court also issued an order precluding the law school from using race as a factor in the admissions process for future cases. University of Michigan Documents Center, *University of Michigan Affirmative Action Lawsuit* accessed at http://www.lib.umich.edu/libhome/Documents.center/umaffirm.html, April 29, 2001. See also "Judge bars Michigan law school admissions on race" accessed at http://www.cnn.com/2001/LAW/03/27/michigan.law.school.02/, April 29, 2001.

6. This information was provided by David Montejano, director of the Center for Mexican American Studies at the University of Texas, Austin. See also Gary R. Hanson and Lawrence Burt, *Responding to Hopwood: Using Policy Analysis Research to Re-design Scholarship Criteria* (Austin: University of Texas at Austin), accessed at www.utexas.edu/student/research/reports/reports.html, August 7, 2000.

CHAPTER 5

HEALTH
CARE

Prescription for Latinos:
No on Prop. 166
**Initiatives: By pressuring small businesses and ignoring community
clinics, the measure would hurt the working poor.**

*Adela de la Torre criticizes Prop. 187, the Save Our State initiative which
would rightly cut many taxpayer-funded services to illegal aliens, for shifting the illegal immigration debate from employment to entitlements. But
one of the reasons why California is in such dire financial straits is precisely because of the large sums spent by the state on illegals. . . . Entitlements for illegals should be addressed, and Prop. 187 is genuine reform
that the public supports, not hysteria.*

—Jeffrey A. Hartwick[1]

HEALTH INSURANCE in the state of California has become an increasing luxury for a precious few in large employer sectors of the
economy. But even there, the continuity of some benefits is being
questioned, as evidenced by the recent announcement of McDonnell

Douglas that retiree health insurance benefits would run only four more years before permanent termination.

For Latinos in California—over 40 percent of whom lack health insurance—the specter is even more grim. More and more Latinos face an increasingly hostile health-care delivery system as state budget cuts threaten the viability of community clinics and county services. A key to unlocking this dilemma for Latinos and others will be the development of a well-thought-out financing scheme to incorporate more of the state's uninsured population, particularly those trapped between poverty and the middle class, that is, the working poor. Although numerous health-care financing measures have been discussed at both the state and federal level, we will have the opportunity November 3 to determine the future of health-care financing and delivery of services for the state.

Concerned with the rising number of uninsured residents, the California Medical Association has placed Proposition 166, the Affordable Basic Health Care Act of 1992, on the ballot. A recent review of the proposition by the Latino Coalition for a Healthy California resulted in an unequivocal thumbs down for this proposal. The key weaknesses cited:

- •Millions of uninsured Latinos and others would stay uninsured, since part-time employees working less than 17.5 hours per week, those working for new employers, independent contractors and the unemployed would not be covered.
- •The regressive financing measures recommended in the initiative would seriously weaken small employers, the major source of employment for Latinos in the state. Costs to businesses have been projected at billions of dollars, most of which would impact small firms. Latino employees would be forced during this severe recession to select between a job or health insurance. Is this a real choice?
- •The recommended benefit package does not provide needed care for the relatively youthful Latino population. For example, preventive services such as family planning and contraception and outpatient medications are not in-

cluded. As the quality of care is decreased for those who can only afford basic coverage, basic benefits will become more substandard.

•The plan does not address the development of community-based health delivery systems, which have served Latinos well. These health centers have relied on piecemeal funding to provide services to the underserved and uninsured. Shifting resources away from the current safety net for Latinos without a proven alternative does not increase access.

•The Health Care Coverage Commission that will oversee the new law consists of twelve members, six appointed by the governor and three each by the assembly speaker and the state Senate. Five of the appointees must represent doctors or hospitals, outweighing the two seats allotted to consumers. No Latinos are included, even though they will be disproportionately affected.

There is no doubt that health-care financing reform is needed. But should we allow something as precious as our children's health to be determined by one special interest group that largely has ignored the health needs of Latinos?

Should Latinos be willing to undermine the community clinics, which though short on staff and dollars, have served us in migrant camps and urban barrios? Should we place the small employers of working-poor Latinos in the unsavory position of trading jobs for health insurance? Finally, should we not have a right, as the largest minority population in the state, to participate in this reform process?

Los Angeles Times, October 22, 1992

Access Is Vital in Health-Care Reform
Language skills and cultural sensitivity are vital if Latinos and others outside the system are to be adequately served.

There is a lady . . . where I work that's a supervisor of the janitorial staff. She's been in the U.S. over twenty years, but is uncomfortable in English and prefers to chat with the Spanish-speakers in our office. To me, . . . [t]his is a specific of the generality of business requiring their public-dealing personnel to be bilingual (which always means Spanish). Why should the Mexico-centric . . . be catered to if "they" know English is the pathway to success?

—*Thomas A. Erskine*

LATINOS IN THE UNITED STATES represent a rapidly growing and diverse population. Among the country's 19.4 million Latinos are Mexicans, Puerto Ricans, Cubans and other Central and South Americans. Geography and political and economic forces have resulted in the Mexican-origin group comprising the largest Latino population in the United States.

More than a third of all U.S. Latinos live in California, as do more than 60 percent of U.S. amnesty applicants under the 1986 Immigration Reform and Control Act. Los Angeles County, with the largest concentration of the state's Latino population and home to half of all the state's amnesty applicants, is also home to thousands of Latinos without health insurance.

According to a recent national study on Latino health-care access by UCLA researcher Robert Valdez, almost four out of ten working-age Latinos do not have health insurance, compared with about one-quarter of blacks and one-seventh of whites. Given these grim statistics, it is not surprising that the states with the largest number of uninsured in the country are California, Texas and Florida—states with large concentrations of Latino workers.

In all three states, most of the Latino uninsured lack employment-based health coverage because, too often, they have jobs in the small-employer labor market, where neither employer nor worker can afford premiums. In addition, eligibility requirements to programs such as Medicaid vary among states, hurting those who live in states with restrictive eligibility requirements.

The stark portrait of dwindling health-care access due to poverty is more bleak for Latinas. For many, the dream of employer-based insurance will never be realized, as daily cash wages provide immediate survival but benefits such as health insurance are reserved for the lucky few. Because they mainly are in low-paying clerical, service and manufacturing jobs, these women can't pay for private health insurance. Thus we find that more than 40 percent of women from Mexico in service-sector jobs do not have health insurance.

Although employment and poverty have often been cited as the key reasons for lack of health insurance for Latinas, other issues become equally significant in understanding why these women do not have health insurance. Recent immigrants from Mexico without much education, who are unmarried and have limited English language skills will have lower rates of public or private health-insurance coverage.

Lack of health insurance for Latinas has potentially devastating consequences. Their higher birthrates indicate a greater need for access to prenatal and postpartum care. Yet many of these women have little or no prenatal care. High rates of teen-age pregnancy, low use of contraception and relatively high rates of cervical cancer compared with non-Latina women are all preventable, but they require immediate intervention to avoid the potentially catastrophic losses to the community.

Piecemeal approaches to address the reproductive health issues of Latinas can no longer ignore these issues and assume that the existing safety net for the poor will adequately meet their health-care needs.

As the Clinton task force announces sweeping reforms for the nation's health-care system, one can only hope that a community health agenda is developed that incorporates Latinas and others who have historically been disenfranchised from the delivery of health-care services. Latinas and others who are marginally attached to the labor force must be included in any new system.

Such reforms must go beyond traditional employer-based programs, and portability of benefits must be guaranteed so no one is locked into an undesirable job because of health-care benefits.

Health-care reform must also include a community health agenda targeted to the needs of the underserved to ensure better use of low-cost preventive services. Access, broadly defined, goes beyond financial access; it requires humanitarian treatment of all patients regardless of income, ethnicity or sex. It demands both financial and educational empowerment of all participants to prevent illness. One step in providing empowerment for Latinas and others who have historically been marginalized is to insist that health professionals have appropriate language skills and cultural sensitivity, as is the case in many community-based clinics in Los Angeles.

As Angelenos anxiously await the recommendations of the Clinton task force, we must recognize that our diverse city will be the gauge that determines success or failure of this program. Our community must actively participate in the reform process so that universal health-care coverage for all becomes more than just a dream.

Los Angeles Times, March 31, 1993

Do We Save Lives or Count Bodies?
If counties can opt out of health services, urban areas will attract even more of the state's poor and uninsured.

Seven million Californians do not have health insurance, and even those who do have coverage are only one serious illness away from financial ruin.

—Rep. Xavier Becerra (D–Los Angeles)[2]

IMAGINE A DIABETIC WITHOUT INSULIN, collapsing and dying on the street because no health provider is willing to give care. This could happen if Assembly Bill (AB) 154 becomes law. The legislation introduced by Assemblyman Bernie Richter (R-Chico) proposes to amend California's welfare code to relieve counties from their current financial burden of providing services for all "incompetent, poor, indigent persons and those incapacitated by age, disease, or accident." County health officers would end up counting bodies instead of saving lives.

The pressure to downsize county health departments is not new and the burden of providing care to growing numbers of uninsured people has outstripped several counties' budgets. Officials in small counties and those most impacted by the downturns in the state's economy resent the intrusiveness of state mandates that they provide this care. The continued bad economy and the realignment of the state budget, which eliminated funding for such county programs, fueled the move to dismantle state mandates. Many county supervisors had to choose between the public safety or public health. Though county health providers recognized the severe limitations of providing services to the indigent, they also recognized the huge social cost of not protecting residents from communicable diseases and destroying the health safety net for the poor.

Steve Thompson of the California Medical Association has criticized AB 154 for departing from California's tradition of requiring counties to be the safety-net providers for their own poor. C. Duane Dauner, president of the California Association of Hospitals and Health Systems, provides a more sobering analysis of the negative effect on California's health system: Immediate impacts, he says, would include reduced access to essential health services, greater incidence of death and disease and shifting of costs from the government to private providers. Critics of this bill share a real fear that large urban counties would become even greater magnets for the uninsured and underinsured. Los Angeles County, with its six large publicly owned hospitals and extensive network of health centers, would be forced to share these limited resources with surrounding counties that opt out of providing services. Los Angeles supervisors would have to choose between further restricting eligibility for needed public-health programs like prenatal care or pressuring the state for more money.

There is no doubt that unfunded and underfunded mandates, both by Congress and by the state legislature, are an issue for county and municipal governments. But we must not be shortsighted in eliminating services for the poor. Infectious diseases like tuberculosis place us all at risk. County health programs are needed not only to monitor the outbreak of these diseases but also to mobilize the state and federal resources for effective treatment. As attractive as private-sector solutions may be, we must remember that government plays an equally important role in providing services when markets fail. Private-sector providers facing greater pressure from lower profit margins cannot absorb all of the indigent. In California, we once wisely decided that all counties must share in this burden because illness and disease do not recognize county boundaries. To allow supervisors the option of not providing services to the poor is to invite chaos, disease and death, a long-run cost we all will share.

Los Angeles Times, February 22, 1995

On Health Care, a Matter of Trust
The Canadian-style plan proposed for California promises health security, but includes job losses and more taxation.

As one of the ninety members of Congress co-sponsoring a single-payer health care reform proposal, I believe that single-payer deserves a more constructive assessment, and not such a doomsday description. When considering the whole picture, the single-payer system holds tremendous appeal to all Californians

—Rep. Xavier Becerra (D-Los Angeles)[3]

AS CONGRESS hammers out its final version of health-care reform, the bipartisan compromise legislation is moving away from radical changes to the current system. As Congress pushes incremental approaches, the focus is on meaningful reform and phase-in strategies to meet President Clinton's goal of universal coverage. The moderate view in Congress may reflect the general shift noted in the recent *Times Mirror* poll that shows public support for employer mandates waning even though the desire for universal coverage remains strong. Oddly, as the pendulum swings to the right in Congress, Californians are swinging left as they open their debate on the single-payer model for health care.

This is not the first time that the state has looked at Canadian-style health-care financing. Since 1990, consumer and physician advocate groups have supported state Sen. Nicholas C. Petris (D-Oakland) in his attempt to get a single-payer system through the legislature. But even though supporters of the single-payer system were able to muster a majority in both the Senate and the Assembly, they were not able to get the required two-thirds vote to pass the legislation. So, Glen Schneider, campaign manager for Californians for Health Security, said, "It was time to place the single-payer model directly in front of the California voters in November."

Comprehensive benefits are proposed under the California Health Security initiative: preventive services, including dental and psychological care, prescription drugs and long-term care. It will keep the familiar private fee-for-service system intact, giving physicians greater control in the delivery of services as well as maintaining existing health-maintenance organizations (HMOs) such as the Kaiser Foundation. Ultimately, whether a fee-for-service provider or an HMO will survive in this new financing scheme will be determined by consumer assessment of quality of care. In addition, the new system promises to eliminate insurance forms. Advocates of the single-payer system believe that if government can efficiently process millions of tax returns, it certainly should be able to pay health providers with equal efficiency.

As ideal as these benefits sound, they come with costs. The costs do not exceed the present costs that we pay for our private and public system, but they do require everyone to contribute their fair share toward universal and comprehensive coverage. The cost of providing universal coverage for all Californians will be about $100 billion. More than half of the revenue would come directly from government programs such as Medicare and MediCal. The rest would be generated by eliminating employer-based premiums and using a payroll tax on employers, a flat 2.5 percent income tax, a 2.5 percent surtax on those who make incomes above $250,000 for individual returns and $500,000 for joint returns and a $1-per-pack tobacco tax.

Taxes alone may frighten many voters away from supporting the initiative, unless they realize that the risk of no coverage or inadequate coverage is potentially more devastating. Other issues will be the windfall savings large employers will receive when they no longer pay health-insurance premiums and whether they will use it to create more jobs. For small and medium employers who have never provided health insurance, the new payroll-tax requirement will create fertile ground for opponents to argue that layoffs are inevitable. Proponents of the initiative agree that there will be an employment impact on the fifty thousand plus private health-insurance employees who will be displaced by the new public system.

There is no doubt that the campaign faces an uphill battle in persuading voters to accept higher taxes as well as potential job loss. Yet dwarfing these issues is persuading the public that government can be trusted to provide these services. Thus far, supporters have built their government efficiency argument on scapegoating the private health-insurance industry. Fraud and waste certainly exist in the private sector, but government-run agencies are definitely not immune from such practices. Furthermore, Americans do not share the Canadians' history of trusting government or placing individual rights subordinate to the collective good. Unless voters can be persuaded that government really works for them, the single-payer initiative will face the same fate as that of any other tax-and-spend proposal come November.

Los Angeles Times, August 17, 1994

For California, an Unhealthy Plan
Relying on Medicare and Medicaid savings has dire implications for states with many on public assistance.

De la Torre raises the issues of cost and higher taxes. The discussion mix should also recognize the savings. According to the General Accounting

Office, the federal auditing agency, a single-payer system in the United States would save close to $100 billion each year. . . . By eliminating burdensome paperwork and other administrative expenses, we cut out the costly middleman. . . . In fact, the Medicare program, which has been managed by the U.S. government for nearly thirty years, spends just 2 percent on administrative costs.

—*Rep. Xavier Becerra (D-Los Angeles)*[4]

PRESIDENT CLINTON'S health-care reform bill promises to revolutionize access to care for millions of uninsured and underinsured Americans. But the voluminous Health Security Act falls short of Clinton's promise of simple guidelines for health-care reform. It would take a task force of lawyers, insurance agents and management experts to explain the three major sections of the act.

Even without this cadre of experts, the weakness of this legislation is obvious. There is no solid financing mechanism to provide the array of health benefits. The enriched benefit package goes far beyond the benefits of most middle-class Americans who have insurance. The current employer-employee partnership of cost-sharing remains, but the bill requires coverage of all Americans. So where do the dollars for those millions who are uninsured and underinsured come from? Much of it is planned from Medicaid and Medicare cost savings. As reasonable as this may sound, it is hardly practical, given the current low rates of reimbursement, which often do not even cover costs. It also has dire implications for states such as California with large numbers of MediCal (Medicaid) enrollees. If MediCal rates of reimbursement are reduced or do not keep up with inflation, the cost-savings strategy from MediCal could create enormous pressure not only on our state budget, but also on counties such as Los Angeles with large numbers of MediCal enrollees.

Although there are additional funds generated from "sin" taxes on alcohol and cigarettes and a 1 percent tax on private-sector purchasing pools, or health alliances, these are decreasing sources of revenue. The latter tax should induce most companies to enroll their employees in regional alliances. The net winners would not be consumers, but large corporations that can shift their rising costs of health care to the federal government.

Another major problem in the Clinton proposal is that consumer choices of providers will be curtailed. With the concentration of buying power through the health alliances, there will be fewer providers. This is because providers will have to assume all the risk of caring for their patients. Now, both providers and insurers share risk for health outcomes. But health alliances will assume no risk, forcing providers into larger delivery systems—mega–HMOs. Over time, traditional fee-for-service providers will be eliminated. The net effect will be a decrease in consumer choice.

And, while the bill authorizes money to speed the coordination of community-based health systems into established health plans, it does not guarantee appropriation of funds. What if Congress decides to pass the law but not provide money for linking our public hospitals and county and community clinics? For Los Angeles, this could undermine a public-health safety net that could not be duplicated in the private sector. Emergency care must still be provided at the county level for all, and this requires adequate support both from the federal and state governments.

These major financing pitfalls, combined with the implications for consumer choice, have shifted significant support away from the bill. Even Sen. Dianne Feinstein (D-Calif.), who is co-sponsoring it, has been at best lukewarm with her endorsement.

Meanwhile, the most popular of the competing plans is the Chafee/Thomas bill, which relies on the current system with no employer mandate. This proposal is leaner in health benefits and allows for restriction of benefits if funding is not available. There are no restrictions based on citizenship or specific limits on co-payments, deductibles or out-of-pocket costs. As in the Clinton proposal, financing relies on the Medicare and Medicaid cost savings as well as caps on tax deductibility of employer-provided health benefits. A more fundamental problem of this bill is that it does not guarantee universal coverage.

Other challenges to the overwritten and underfunded Clinton proposal are springing up. If Clinton is to seriously push forward, he must begin to pare down his bloated benefits package, provide choice of providers to the middle class and develop real means of funding for states like California. Clinton's package will falter if it does not answer these issues soon. Few can quibble with the need for universal and affordable health care, but we must provide a solid financial base for equitable reform.

Los Angeles Times, February 2, 1994

Hear My Story, Know My Pain
Women who have had abortions must speak out to put a face on choice and retain it as an option.

I was in college in the 1960s. Abortion was illegal. I found myself pregnant and not ready to have a baby . . . I went with the "Dr." and was dropped off at a shopping center, picked up by two men and driven to an apartment . . . they made me take off my clothes and took pictures of me . . . They proceeded to give me a painful abortion . . . one month later I started having horrible stomach cramps in the middle of the night . . . I started bleeding. The Dr. at the hospital did emergency surgery and tried to fix the brutal abortion I was given a month before. I say to women and men please don't lose your choice. It could be your daughter. If abortion becomes illegal it doesn't stop the procedure . . . I've never shared this with anyone.
—Anonymous Reader

Great column this morning! It's a fitting antidote to the many so called pro-lifers who, having had abortions, later decide (after they've escaped an unwanted pregnancy!) that abortions are wrong. Especially when people other than them need to have one.
—Karen Grigsby Bates

AS THE SENATE considers the nomination of Dr. Henry Foster to be surgeon general, few political commentators have focused on the importance of these hearings for the civil rights of all women. Women must begin to regain control over the abortion debate by using what we all have in our control: our stories. We must give voice to the pain of the past and speak our minds at home, at work and in our churches and synagogues. We must show our friends, our spouses and our children the human face of choice and abortion. If we fear the consequences of our narratives, the religious right will continue to dictate our moral code and our choices.

My story begins fifteen years ago. I was in the last stages of my graduate career at UC Berkeley. Only a few months remained before I would defend my thesis. Nights turned into days as I lived in the graduate student office with my colleagues, studying, preparing, anticipating the trick questions that would be posed by our faculty tormentors. As the anxiety mounted, I became sleepless, edgy and increasingly run down, until one day I realized that my food had an odd taste and my fatigue was mounting daily. I knew it was time to go the student health center when I fell asleep as I was talking with a friend.

As I waited for the doctor to call my name, I closed my eyes and dreamed of the day that I would walk across that stage. The elusive Ph.D. that had taken so many years would finally be in my grandmother's and my mother's hands. It was my favorite dream, one that I played over and over in my mind whenever I thought I could go no further.

Adela de la Torre! I woke up and entered the sterile room. A young doctor gently queried me on my symptoms. She listened carefully and took copious notes, and at the end paused to ask: "Do you think you may be pregnant?" Without a moment's hesitation, I replied, "That's impossible, I have a Dalkon shield IUD. I just had it checked. There is no way that I could be pregnant."

I was wrong. I had a week to decide. Pregnancy with the IUD in place would risk my life or fetal damage. Removing it would abort the fetus. I had no health insurance, no full-time job and I was a month away from completing my graduate career. I screamed, I wept. This wasn't fair. This could not happen to me.

But it did. As the nurse held my hand, a doctor explained to me what was about to transpire. As he suctioned, a scream leapt from the depths of my soul. It seemed like an eternity passed, but it was merely seconds.

Alarmed, the nurse stepped back. Instinctively, the doctor grasped my hand, sharing for that moment the pain that I felt. As he wiped the tears from my face, he showed me human compassion, compassion that does not judge the painful choices that others make, but helps to heal the wounds.

My life has moved on since that springtime day when my world stopped. Not without regret, but with the peace of mind that I made the right choice. A choice that I will never forget, but one that was mine to make. As I tell my daughters my story, they fear such a choice. But as young women, they know that the responsibility to choose is not free from pain. They do not like their mother's choice, but they have accepted it with the willingness to understand and the compassion to forgive.

As the moral arbiters in Congress begin to grill Foster on his credibility, let us also demand a human face to the stories of those women who sought care from this physician from rural Tennessee. Let us see if these great senators have the courage to hear poor black women tell their stories of why they made their choices. What dreams did they put on hold? I have no doubt that we will weep when we hear their stories, but we also will begin to understand what abortion really means for poor women. For decades, women have whispered their stories and felt the pain. Isn't it time we begin to heal ourselves from these wounds?

Los Angeles Times, May 17, 1995

Access to Health Care in the Twenty-First Century

Perhaps no other article was more painful to write than the article about my abortion. This is, perhaps, one of the most private matters in the life of any woman. Few women who have had abortions forget this traumatic experience, and the public debate continually reminds them of their vilified status in American society. For Mexican-origin women who are Catholic, this dilemma creates even more emotional havoc. At the same time, women who have benefited from this basic right need to make public their painful experiences in order to protect the rights of their children as well as the reproductive rights of all women.

Why did I share this very personal event in my life? I do not want to suggest that abortions are either common or accepted in the Mexican American community based only on my personal experience. However, I feel it is important to recognize that even though Mexican Americans may only whisper about this personal tragedy, it occurs in our community more often than we would like to think. The trigger for me was the heated debated over Clinton's surgeon general nominee, Dr. Henry Foster, an African-American physician who had provided abortions to low-income African-American women in Alabama. This issue surfaced during the confirmation hearings as a reason not to support his appointment. Although this was not the sole reason for the opposition to his appointment as surgeon general, it reveals the contradictory attitudes of the conservative Christian establishment with respect to the human rights of the poor, particularly women of color. Having been in a situation where I financially could not afford an abortion, there were no alternatives for me except a state-subsidized abortion. Moreover, mine was a high-risk pregnancy due to the presence of a Dalkon Shield in my womb, which created enormous health risks to both the fetus and me. Thus, I was forced to make a quick decision to avoid possible death or damage to my fetus. Due to their religious convictions, for many individuals this is no excuse for having an abortion, nor would they condone my decision to have premarital sex. Nonetheless, it reflects the choice that I made and the right that all women should have despite their economic status. As a direct beneficiary of this important right, I felt it was incumbent on me to share my experience with the many readers of the *Los Angeles Times* in defense of Dr. Foster and the service he provided to poor black women in the South. Compassionate physicians like Dr. Foster are the individuals who make this horrific decision more bearable, and they should not be penalized for providing this service. Unfortunately, even today, the right to an abortion is still under attack by the conservative right, and there is an even greater need for women of all colors to speak out despite public retribution.

Beyond the emotional aspects of the abortion debate lie fundamental issues regarding access to quality health care. Most of my commentaries have focused on access issues, as this was and still is the primary health problem affecting the Latino community, particularly the Mexican-origin community. In California, the Latino population is made up largely of immigrant groups from Mexico and Central America, and it has the highest uninsured rate in the state. Initiatives like Proposition 166, the Affordable Basic Health Care Act of 1992, which attempted to provide greater access to the uninsured populations of California, reflect just one strategy to address the issue of the growing uninsured population. Although it failed, subsequent policy initiatives focusing on programs such as Medicaid and reforms to existing public-health delivery systems generally use strategies that extend the safety net for uninsured Latinos. However, a major problem during the latter part of the 1990s and continuing today is the job placement of most Latinos, which is primarily in the small business sector. This sector is vulnerable since it does not have the resource base to provide cost-effective health insurance. At the same time, many of the strategies that were suggested during the 1990s to force small businesses to provide health insurance did not contain sufficient financial support for these employers to incorporate mandated health insurance programs for uninsured workers. Thus, the debate was about sustaining jobs within the ethnic enclave economy or providing health care. This debate has not been resolved, as evidenced by the continued reliance on publicly subsidized health care. Nevertheless, the access issue must be resolved as means of improving the health status of future generations of Latinos.

Policy discussions for the next decade will continue to focus on how to improve access and how to provide access to high quality care. The issue of providing quality care to this diverse group surfaces in the discussions of implementing culturally competent health-care services and evaluating these services with respect to health-care outcomes. Cultural competency includes both proficient linguistic skills and cultural sensitivity, and it may well become the driving force in developing the curricular content used in educating new health-care professionals. Emotional issues like abortion and the ability of Latinas to make their own individual choices require physicians and health-care providers to understand their patients' cultural background. This is a key component to compassionate care. Obviously, this may not address the broader moral argument surrounding abortion, but it does address the reality of this issue among many low-income Latinas.

Notes

1. Jeffrey A. Hartwick, "Immigration Initiative," *Los Angeles Times,* July 22, 1994, home edition, metro, sec. B, p. 6.

2. Xavier Becerra, "Single-Payer Health Reform," *Los Angeles Times,* August 26, 1994, home edition, metro, sec. B, p. 6.

3. Ibid.

4. Ibid.

CHAPTER 6

WELFARE
REFORM
AND THE
UNDERCLASS

To Aid Welfare Children at Risk, Take Them Away to Safe Havens
Their needs should come first, ahead of neglectful parents' rights.
This would be true reform of a dysfunctional system.

I just finished your remarkable op-ed piece in the Los Angeles Times, *"To*

Aid Welfare Children at Risk . . . " and felt I had to write you. It is bril-

liant! I am particularly taken with your focus on the welfare of children,

not the people who happen to produce them, and the range of suggestions

for reform you propose.

—Anthony Pascal

ENDING POVERTY in America must rely on programs that reinforce individual fortitude. Those who lack this moral backbone will soon become the undeserving poor. As with other political mandates, rich in rhetoric and piecemeal solutions, ideology that describes the poor is central to the mission of gaining popular acceptance for welfare reform. This is precisely why the imagery of the welfare mother on the dole and the deadbeat dad becomes so powerful in the national welfare debate: It allows us to simplify whom we are willing to support during times of economic duress and whom we are willing to let go. It also allows us to ignore the truly invisible and voiceless poor of America, the children.

Yet daily we are bombarded with the reality of these children—in the media, in the streets and in our schools. The drug-exposed infants, the sexually and physically abused, the runaway and throwaway children. They become victims of the trickle-down welfare programs targeted to their parents—policies that place the biological entitlement of the parent as the major determinant on the quality of life for the child. Thus, if we deem the parent unfit to receive welfare support, the child, too, loses.

To propel the welfare debate in a new direction, we need to decouple the link between biological parent and child. This is crucial not only for determining needs, but also for determining appropriate public strategies. We have examples of programs that do this: school meals, health care for poor children. But there is little coordination, and funding relies increasingly on the benevolence of policy-makers. We also need to shift our focus away from parents toward society's responsibility. As difficult as it is to accept that parents may not love or be able to care for their children, we must stop eulogizing the loss of "the family" and trying to re-create it through federal policy. The crisis in the family cuts across society, but poor children are at greater risk.

All children must have an alternative when the family environment is disruptive or destructive to their personal well-being. For example, a recent study by the Children's Defense Fund illustrated that the Los Angeles County Department of Children's Services had open files on approximately one-fourth of all the children who died in 1989; more than one in five of these cases had confirmed reports of domestic violence in the household. How many other children in Los Angeles survived 1989 and the brutality of their family life, and how much longer will we act as accomplices to a failed state and federal welfare policy that places parental rights above children's rights?

Consider the possibility of abused or neglected children having the option of living in a residential school or community home. Here, we could marshal our resources to buffer these children from the violence of poverty and abuse. We could also avoid duplication of services. Residential programs would provide a nurturing and secure environment where children do not have to witness the daily degradation of their parents, withstand verbal or physical abuse or fear going to school. They would allow older children and hard-to-place children who are removed from their homes to avoid the heartbreak of the revolving door of foster care, where their dreams of a permanent home are rarely realized. They would also alleviate the pressure from a foster-care system where inadequate regulation puts children at greater risk of future abuse. School districts could coordinate after-school care for those with learning disabilities or special needs with residential programs. Social workers, physical therapists, nutritionists and educators could help rebuild self-esteem and hope for these children. Parents who are not abusive should maintain their rights of contact with their children, but we should recognize that the parents' needs are secondary.

Our current policy has not created greater equality and economic security for our children. With every round of welfare reform, we resurrect the image of the family and parental responsibility as the cornerstone for alleviating poverty. We assume that by infusing our morality into parents, it will trickle down to the children. It is time to bury our family rhetoric and examine and respect the individual rights of children. It requires us to look beyond the umbilical cord to create a meaningful future for our youth.

Los Angeles Times, December 29, 1993

Compassionate Welfare Reform
Training and loans help the poor become successful entrepreneurs rather than recipients of public assistance.

My central ideas, I think, are highly complementary to those you expressed

in your article. I am particularly impressed by the damages, actual physi-

cal damages, done to children by such parents as a result of prenatal sub-

stance abuse, bad nutrition and lack of maternal health care, and abuse,

neglect and poor parenting once the kids are born. These practices result

in "cursed" children, so disadvantaged physically, mentally, and emotion-

ally that they will never find a secure place in American society but merely

go on to perpetuate the cycle of joblessness, crime, teenage conception

and dependency.

—Anthony Pascal

IN THIS ERA of partisan politics, it is refreshing to see that Los Angeles has a group of women who have developed a concrete and effective welfare reform strategy. The Coalition for Women's Economic Development (CWED) strives to get people off the welfare roll by providing technical assistance and small loans so that poor people can start their own businesses.

Although CWED does not discriminate on the basis of race or sex, 83 percent of the participants are women. Its clients are from Central City, Watts, Echo Park, Pico Union, Inglewood and South Gate—areas with some of the highest poverty rates in southern California.

How has CWED made inroads into a client base that most commercial banks shun? Most banks view the issues of collateral or poor credit as the greatest stumbling block for low-income entrepreneurs. CWED views the lack of technical knowledge as the biggest barrier to their clients' success in maintaining small businesses. CWED also recognizes that as long as private financial institutions expect the poor to have assets beyond their wages, small business loans will never be within their reach. That is why CWED focuses on the potential for a successful business, combined with concrete business skill training. All participants in this lending and training program are required to participate in business workshops that focus on management, credit and peer lending.

A significant amount of CWED's budget, therefore, goes to training and follow-up technical support to its "microbusiness" loan recipients. This strategy of coupling training with lending is a risk management tool; it minimizes the chance of loan defaults and small business failure.

Last year, eighty-two microbusinesses participated in CWED's Solidarity Circle program. The idea behind this program evolved from the Grameen bank in Bangladesh, where poor women were given the opportunity to borrow by sharing their risk with others like them and providing mutual support. Similarly, CWED's program brings together five small business owners, providing them with the requisite technical assistance and training before reviewing their loan applications. The average loan approved last year was $2,294. As no collateral is required for these loans, the group assumes responsibility if any of its members defaults.

The value of CWED to inner city community development has not gone unnoticed by the mayor's office and major corporate sponsors. Last year, the Los Angeles Community Development Department provided $176,082 to CWED. That was matched by contributions from private foundations such as Irvine, Pacific Telesis, Bank of America, Ms. and First Interstate Bank.

Yet CWED today is at a crossroads, deciding whether to maintain its microbusiness loans or to focus on loans to more established small businesses, which do not require the high level of technical assistance and training from the staff. CWED Executive Director Mari Riddle agrees with those who say that the focus on microbusiness loans, although costly, must not be abandoned even for greater economic security.

CWED and other microloan programs show that the major stumbling block to effective lending to the poor is the lack of technical assistance, not the availability of loan dollars. It would make sense for the Los Angeles Community Development Bank, with its focus on lending in empowerment zones and low-income areas, to partner with established groups such as CWED. They could provide the financial and technical support to offset the high transaction costs of lending to poor people with no collateral—an economically sound and compassionate strategy for welfare reform.

Los Angeles Times, August 9, 1995

Failing Our Children

Rescuing Lives without Hope
Smaller classes, sports programs, jobs, church involvement: These are possible solutions to juvenile crime.

[Y]our article . . . was true . . . you wrote my story of life . . . I was sixteen years young, now I am forty-four and I have no future. I was in high school for a minute, before I was expelled for truancy. I only had one place to go to without parents . . . the Barrio . . . and friends "Homies." . . . We had no hope . . . this is all I know, . . . I had committed murder at seventeen, and on my way to San Quentin, I learned how to use and sell drugs while their [sic]! I have seen my homies die and get life in prison. It's a revolving door for me, in and out. And I just keep on seeing these guys in here (jail) are younger and younger also illiterate, no education, and they are mostly laughing their heart out. But shedding many tears at night.

—Alfredo R. Bryan

HIS PIERCING BROWN EYES told a story beyond his smile. At seventeen, he was in jail for smoking "bud" (marijuana). He had not a single unit of high school credit, and his goal for ten years from now was to be high and not get caught. Another youth, whose smooth baby face masked a bitter cynicism, forecast his adult world as life behind bars with his dad. An unusual strategy for finding an absent father. But perhaps most heart wrenching was a boy no older than fourteen who saw prison and violent death as his inevitable fate. These youths represent many children of color, who disproportionately fill our prisons.

I had met them in a group activity area for violent juvenile offenders. I saw no books there, no posters, no computers—no tools that would allow them to grow as human beings and as skilled adults. The one classroom in the facility could at best serve only 20 of the

130—50 over capacity—juvenile detainees. The facility had become so overcrowded that children slept on mats on the cafeteria floor. What are the prospects for these children who are dropping out of our schools and their families? We have offered them tough love and zero tolerance, but this has had little effect. One youth, on being sent to the center, had remarked, "At least in jail, I can sober up and have three meals before going back into the streets." So much for deterrence.

Americans should not be surprised that we are failing in our war against juvenile crime. We are failing because the environment these children live in is far worse than any deterrent thus offered. For example, as a society we support zero tolerance of violence in our public schools, but how does that translate in real life? We kick out of school those most in need of education and counseling, and they land on the highest crime and drug-infested streets. The "homies" become their family and network for survival and educational training. As they drop into slanging and banging, they move further away from homeroom and football. They become the mean criminals and thugs we hate and believe we can control with further violence to their self-esteem.

We are creating a growing underclass in American society, one that is disproportionately nonwhite and poor. They are our native sons and daughters who are poor. They are our native sons and daughters who are filling courtrooms and jails. They have a separate language, a separate culture, and a separate dream. They are not in our schools because they cannot survive there. As one boy said to me, "The only thing that gets us respect is fear. Being a Mafioso or like Scarface, what could be better than that?" Dying for a friend, defending your turf or grabbing a bat and beating someone who makes you mad are reasonable choices for these youth.

So what do we do beyond creating more prisons and building higher walls around our homes and communities? Perhaps we begin by listening to those children who have hope. I asked these kids what would make a difference in their lives, and beyond the bravado they had concrete solutions for deterring juvenile criminal behavior.

Several agreed that they would have had a better chance if their public school classes were smaller and more teachers had encouraged them. If they had a place to play sports after school or if schools would stop taking sports away when their grades dropped, they could play football or basketball and maybe even go to college. If they had jobs in their neighborhoods and someone to guide them to do the right thing, it would make a difference. If churches got involved, they would be able to become closer to God. If they knew that once they graduated from high school there might be financial assistance for college, they would reach for that dream.

Simply put, many of our most violent children know that they need to succeed. They just don't think that it's possible, and we have not given them any indication that we care. We must convince these children that success is possible for them and that we care about their future. We need to develop concrete action plans at the neighborhood level. This requires putting aside our prejudices and fears and working together to shift the tide of juvenile violence and incarceration.

Our schools, our churches, our families and our courts are failing, and our children know this. Isn't it time we become honest with ourselves?

Los Angeles Times, June 18, 1997

Our Disposable Youth and Welfare Reform

Here I am again facing a lifetime in prison for what the government itself is largely responsible for. How can society expect prisoners to conform to its social etiquette when its own government is reducing us to anthropoids, sort of speak, by subjecting selective prisoners to a punishment that is tantamount to torture. This, by large, is happening to Chicano/ Mexicanos and Africanos whom currently occupy 90 percent of the security housing units in California. It's a governmental hate crime! A discretely, and cunningly cruel form of ethnic cleansing.

—Hector Gallegos

DURING THE LAST DECADE of the twentieth century, we may very well be judged positively for our success in sustained economic growth, but harshly for how we treated our youth and the extreme poor. Hector Gallegos, who served ten years at Pelican Bay Prison in California in its isolated security housing unit and is currently facing a life sentence, epitomizes the prisoners who know the gross inhumanity of our criminal justice system. As an individual who wasted his youth in these state warehouses for the poor, his bitterness is a natural outgrowth of being ignored early in his life. His revolving path of violence and incarceration could have been prevented by a caring community.

The practice of criminalizing youth, particularly minority youth, has resulted in much harsher sentences for young people, with both Democrats and Republicans vying for the privilege of destroying a generation of children. For example, passage of the Gang Violence and Juvenile Crime Prevention Act of 1998 (Proposition 21), which reduced the age for sentencing juveniles as adults to as young as fourteen, exemplifies the bipartisan support for criminalizing youth. This initiative, authored by former California Governor Pete Wilson, a Republican, and supported by Democratic Governor Grey Davis, played on unfounded fears of juvenile violence, which had declined significantly between 1993 and 1997. By 1997, youth under eighteen were responsible for only 27 percent of all serious violent crimes.[1] Unfortunately, the targets of this type of reactionary legislation are poor minority youth. As another California prisoner, Alfredo R. Bryan, indicates:

> Today, it's gotten way out of hand. The juveniles are coming in here now with longer sentences, they are found to be unfit as juveniles at fifteen, and sixteen, seventeen, tried in adult court, convicted and brought up here to prison for twenty, twenty-five and more with life tops. Why has it gotten worse? . . . the system has gotten into being a business for institutions. Lock em up and let us work in jails, prisons, industries . . . the system has grown tremendously, from nine state prisons in 1986 to thirty-three state prisons in California in the 1990s. Now what else is new!

What else is new is that the nation's criminal justice system is beginning to be scrutinized by the public because of the racialized nature of how justice is delivered. In a recent American Civil Liberties Union (ACLU) ad in the *New York Times,* this racial imagery was captured by a stark picture of a young African-American teenager surrounded by an editorial about the brutalization and murder of young people of color in prison.[2] This lack of humanity is captured by prison *veterano* Alfredo Bryan in his observation of prison life today, where younger prisoners stand a greater chance of being locked up longer:

> We haven't got much hope for a future for these new generation kids I see here in prison, they are here with ten to twenty years to serve at 80 percent of their sentence without getting into any disciplinary infractions or breaking rules. But you know and I know that these are impossible for them. Kids will break rules, and if they are serving 80–85 percent of their sentence of ten years that's eight and a half years to serve of ten years. They ain't going to make it out. And then many of them have one or two strikes in their history. With a strike and a new beef! Another felony, they can be given double their sentence: which means twenty or more years added. . . . these prisons are full of twenty, nineteen and eighteen years old prisoners. They haven't had a chance at life . . . Who is responsible for our kids . . . ?

Alfredo points to youth who have dropped out of school, who live in substandard housing and severely dysfunctional families, and who are being held to a higher standard than any previous generation in American society. Because we have not aggressively invested in prevention programs that would help increase their resiliency to their harsh environment, we suffer the consequences of a juvenile justice system that criminalizes and destroys young people. The treatment of juvenile offenders, including lack of intervention and rehabilitation, becomes even more lethal for minority adults in our state prisons. The gross inequalities inherent in the criminal justice system can be seen in how we administer the death penalty, which disproportionately affects African Americans and Latinos.

The 2000 presidential election captured the growing discomfort of the American public with the unequal application of the death penalty. This discomfort was visible in the presidential debates about the media's focus on the "compassionate" nature of President George W. Bush, former governor of Texas, who oversaw his state's 136th execution during his tenure as governor. Since the reinstatement of the death penalty in 1976, Texas has led the nation in executions of death row inmates, most of whom are poor or minority. As of July 2000, Texas had 102 Latino inmates remaining on death row. Other states, such as Illinois, however, have placed a moratorium on state executions because of the biased nature of the criminal justice system.[3] The potential consequences of killing innocent inmates because of lack of equal access to a proper defense has troubled not only the public, but also elected leaders. President Clinton stopped federal executions to further investigate the fairness of the judicial process, despite the fact that he does support the death penalty. Thus, at the beginning of the twenty-first century, criminal justice has emerged as a social justice issue that disproportionately affects the Latino and African-American communities.

When President Clinton passed the Personal Responsibility and Work Opportunity Act of 1996, many Democrats viewed this as more of a Republican strategy for welfare reform than a Democratic policy. Clearly, the Clinton Administration was extremely adept at co-opting Republican initiatives, but this success came with a price. That is, many of the issues surrounding equity for the poor, the disenfranchised and the marginalized were ignored, shifting the debate away from a minimum standard of living for the poor to individual responsibility for self-reliance without government intervention.

The legacy of the Clinton Administration may very well be the shift away from the federal-state partnership to support low-income and disabled Americans to one of individual self-reliance. At the same time that this partnership shifted, so too did the nation's demographics. States like California, which today are majority non-white, and other southwestern states with rapidly growing Latino populations used their formidable minority political presence to force local and state government officials to piece together policies that would keep in place the fragile safety net of public services and public education for low-income Latinos. The rapidly growing Mexican-American population, with a large low-income immigrant base, was particularly vulnerable during this period, as the attack on immigrants was growing at the same time that they needed support. This is not a new phenomenon, as all immigrant groups need government support in order to assimilate more rapidly into the broader society and U.S. economy.

In the wake of this ideological shift in the political arena from large, federally subsidized welfare programs to more localized solutions to address welfare reform, communities developed creative strategies for economic development. An excellent example of this was the Coalition for Women's Economic Development (CWED). By helping low-income women in the highest risk communities in Los Angeles and providing them with working capital and technical assistance, CWED was an important model of how to empower minority women in the urban core. Another model emerging from the nonprofit grassroots community was the United Way's support of vouchers for low-income women to help them with transportation costs and purchasing used cars. These types of programs allow low-income women to meet the federal welfare requirement for transitioning into the paid workforce. Many local programs provide focused support that fosters the economic success of the poor, particularly of low-income women.

Another pressing problem not adequately addressed by welfare reform is the problem of severely dysfunctional families. Our failure to address this issue is reflected in my commentary on safe havens for children. It may not be politically correct to criticize parental rights; however, at what point are we going to recognize the rights of psychologically and physically abused children? Ultimately, we need to realize that children are not violent or destructive by nature. Their environment creates the impetus for violent behavior. There needs to be a middle ground between the home and the courts for these children, a safe haven where they can be supported and nurtured.

Notes

1. Office of Juvenile Justice and Delinquency Programs (OJJDP), "Violence by Juveniles, 1973–1997," accessed at http://ojjdp.ncjrs.org/ojstatbb/qa135.html, July 25, 2000.

2. *The New York Times*, July 9, 2000, Advertisement ACLU.

3. Patricia Guadalupe, "Texas Executes Another Latino Prisoner, 'Ethnic Crime Propensity' Issue Remains," *Hispanic Link Weekly Report* 18 (July 3, 2000): 1.

CHAPTER 7

THE EMERGING
DEBATES IN
LOS ANGELES
POLITICS

Have Latinos Matured Politically?
Who can best represent all the people of a district is more important
than the color of a candidate's skin.

Most of the democratic countries of the world use some form of propor-

tional representation . . . such systems usually enhance minority represen-

tation, whether it be ethnic or political. . . . Disenfranchisement and voter

apathy are two sides of the same coin.

—*Ralph J. Ortolano, Jr.*

FEW ANGELENOS outside of the 45th Assembly District in East
Los Angeles had heard of Bill Mabie until a couple of months ago
when Democratic Assemblyman Richard Polanco, now running for
the state Senate, recommended Mabie for his Assembly seat. What
should have passed as merely another political green light from one
incumbent to his favorite son soon became an ugly brawl between
those who deem the 22nd District a "Chicano" seat and those who

recognize ethnicity as only one variable in determining representation. Polanco said his endorsement of Mabie (D) over other, Latino, candidates was due to Mabie's superior qualifications and his ability to best represent the district. But is Polanco's endorsement an honest appraisal? Or is he grandstanding in his state Senate bid?

As Polanco's district director for the past three years, Mabie has worked closely with the community. He has been involved in getting jobs for youth at the housing projects of Ramona Gardens and in revitalizing the Northeast Los Angeles Christmas parade. His success at this grassroots level may very well come from his experience as a Peace Corps volunteer in Central America, where he learned that greater social change can only occur when those in power listen to individual needs. Once this happens, an individual can garner the trust and commitment from the community to support needed change.

Mabie has also gone beyond the 45th District in addressing major concerns of the Latino community with regard to both immigration and citizenship issues. He worked as Polanco's key adviser in developing the California Latino Legislative Caucus immigration policy. Mabie was also directly involved with bills that addressed the Immigration and Naturalization Service (INS) backlog of citizenship applications from legal permanent residents.

So why are both Mabie and Polanco viewed as traitors by many Latino political brokers? First and foremost, there are still many Latinos who buy into a cultural nationalism that blinds them from issues of competency and character. In other words, they have internalized their own oppression to such a point that they have become racists toward non-Latinos.

Second, there are those who fail to recognize that even in so-called Chicano districts, there still is diversity. About two-thirds of the 45th District is Latino, for example, but only a little over 12 percent of the Latinos are registered to vote. The district is about 20 percent Asian American, 2.5 percent African American and the rest white. Thus, this "Chicano" district includes other segments of society whose needs must be met by whoever is elected to the Assembly.

Third, many myopic Latino activists do not recognize that Latino elected officials are increasingly able to go beyond designated Latino districts to capture non-Latino districts as well as broader state offices. Assemblyman Joe Baca (D-San Bernadino) and Cruz Bustamante (Fresno) are embraced by the wider community because they are their districts' best representatives. Crossover votes will determine the outcome in both Polanco's race for the 24th state Senate District in Los Angeles and Sen. Art Torres' race for insurance commissioner. Many of these crossover Latino politicians are emerging as leaders of inter-ethnic coalition building. Their statements increasingly echo the move away from narrow, ethnicity-based politics. Thus Polanco is articulating the new boundaries of Latino politics in the state when he says that "the price of leadership is not knee-jerk responses simply based on skin color or ethnicity, rather now more than ever we need to define the content of a candidate's character and the qualities of the candidate." Latino districts are a beginning but not an end to Latino political empowerment.

If Mabie replaces Polanco as representative of the 45th District, it will be a transition point for Latino districts that reflects the political maturation of this community. By unlocking our political borders to new people who represent our interests, we can relinquish the crudest measure of anyone's worth—the color of their skin. We also can begin to participate in a broader political agenda that abandons reprisals for breaking ethnic ranks and celebrates individuals who share a common vision for social change.

Los Angeles Times, April 20, 1994

When an 85 Percent No-Show Vote Wins
At-large voting for the L.A. Community College Board disenfranchises and discourages most of the community it serves.

I read with interest your article about the Los Angeles Community College District election. . . . I empathize with you. Despite all our efforts, all but two Los Angeles television stations chose to ignore the voters of our District, without so much as reporting the vote totals.

—Ralph J. Ortolano, Jr.

NEXT WEEK, Angelenos will have the opportunity to elect new members to the Los Angeles Community College District Board of Trustees. Unlike both the California State University Board of Trustees and the University of California Board of Regents, community college trustees are elected, not political, appointments. For many voters, this merits little attention or concern. Even though the budgets of community colleges surpass the general revenue of several cities, voter apathy is the rule. Given that this is an off-year election, turnout could be as low as in 1991, when 15 percent of the eligible voters went to the polls. Los Angeles District may be the largest community college district in the nation, with total revenue of $268 million, but it is still controlled by only a handful of voters.

Despite the scant public interest, the community college system is vital to the health of higher education in the state. Community colleges enroll about 60 percent of all students in public higher education, and each district has become a sort of Ellis Island that determines entry into California's elite four-year institutions. Moreover, the demographics of community colleges are rapidly mirroring the demographics of public schools throughout the state: increasingly nonwhite and ethnically diverse. In the Los Angeles Community College District, almost three out of four students are nonwhite; almost 40 percent of the student population is Latino.

Key management issues will face the Los Angeles trustees over the next several years, including balancing access to higher education promised in the state's Master Plan for Higher Education with the threat of shrinking budgets; high projected retirements of full-time faculty within the next fifteen years and the need to plan for qualified replacements; the pressure of increased racial and ethnic polarization of faculty, staff and students; and the growing strain of balancing the need for remedial education with the curriculum requirements of all students. Those elected as trustees should not only represent the interests of the voters, but also be well versed in these problem areas.

Unfortunately, the recent board makeup illustrates that few of those elected are grounded in higher education. Half of the current board members are lawyers, and few have substantive experience in higher education administration or full-time teaching. Many candidates see the board as a stepping-stone for higher office. Past trustees include former Governor Jerry Brown, former District Attorney Ira Reiner, Supervisor Michael Antonovich, and Assembly-woman Gwen Moore.

Moreover, the board is one of the last vestiges of an at-large system of elections, so there are no geographic links to representation and no limits to the number of representatives elected from a particular area of the district. At-large elections disenfranchise ethnic and racial minorities by diluting their voting strength, and greater financial leverage is required to win a citywide or countywide election. Poorer communities are less likely to advance candidates to elected office in an at-large system.

Critics argue that most of the current trustees would not be reelected if there were single-member districts. The influence of narrow special interests that dominate this election, such as the powerful faculty union, would be balanced with that of those who use Los Angeles community colleges. Candidates who have successfully run at-large also would be forced to go beyond their individual pocketbooks and assess whether they can authentically represent a specific constituency.

For ethnic minorities in the district, a shift away from the current at-large system for the community college district may signal that, despite Proposition 187, there is a commitment that no group be excluded and that all are equal participants in determining the future of higher education for the next century.

Los Angeles Times, April 5, 1995

Perspectives on the Mayor's Race:
Whose Vision Equals Greater Los Angeles?
The two candidates must articulate specific, workable programs for the whole area if Los Angeles is to prosper.

Clearly, the message that we received was that the residents of Watts, Carson, Compton, Harbor City, Wilmington, West and South Long Beach don't count, as far as the Hollywood news directors are concerned. Perhaps it is because the population of this district is over 50 percent Latino.

Perhaps it is because it is perceived as a largely African American District.

Certainly it is not because the demographics of our District are similar to

the ethnic origins of the "chosen people" who run Hollywood.

—Ralph J. Ortolano, Jr.

TUESDAY'S ELECTION RESULTS were hardly surprising for most Angelenos, despite rather lackluster campaigns by both Michael Woo and Richard Riordan. Now the real challenge begins, for each must capture the imagination of the voters to become the urban architect to lead us into the twenty-first century. Unfortunately, the campaign rhetoric of both camps has been short on substance and long on emotional appeal.

Does Riordan really believe that his "tough" posture will lead to the economic revival of Los Angeles? Should we view the city as the petulant child who requires the forceful hand of the benevolent patriarch to ensure proper maturation? Will his appeal to the disaffected middle class unify a city torn by racial and ethnic strife? Can an economic strategy that promotes downsizing of government and increased reliance on the invisible hand of market forces promote economic development that is inclusive of all Angelenos?

Will Woo's plea for inclusive politics go beyond the traditional Democratic payback mentality, where window dressing for diversity is substituted for true sharing of power? Can his suggestion of a business-loan program requiring $5 million in city funds to entice private lenders to provide $100 million of new business loans be targeted to minority small businesses to encourage the revitalization of the urban core? Or—as stated by many of his critics—do his ideas reflect extravagant promises proffered to garner the diverse liberal voting blocs needed for election?

What is not clear from either of the candidates is an economic blueprint for a city drowning in a deficit reaching to almost a quarter of its budget, staggering under the weight of a school system with a $400-million deficit and mired by increased division between the poor and the privileged.

As obvious as these problems are, they require each candidate to put aside the partisan rhetoric and imagery and present an economic plan that will truly engender a public dialogue. For example, if Riordan perceives that a more user-friendly city hall will stimulate private investment and employment in the city, why not present his case illustrating the impacts of such a policy on specific segments of the city? The public should be able to discern who are the beneficiaries and whether his strategy will enhance the political and economic life of Los Angeles. Furthermore, his plan should include how his economic policies will provide the necessary tax revenue and budget reductions to ensure fiscal viability.

Similarly, Woo needs to clearly define his redevelopment strategy. As he has positioned himself as the champion of those who have been marginalized from the city's economy and the broader public, he needs to articulate how areas such as South-Central—where almost 40 percent of the residents have annual incomes less than fifteen thousand dollars, more than 25 percent of the households are on public assistance and almost half the residents over twenty-five do not have a high school education—will benefit from his policies. As noble as it is to champion the causes of these individuals, there must be substantive policy to reverse the economic balkanization of the city. Mobilizing the necessary public- and private-sector actors requires Woo to go beyond business as usual for liberal Democrats, which is mouthing piecemeal reform and pointing fingers. He must develop a comprehensive economic strategy and discuss redistribution policies that can garner taxpayers' support.

Both candidates must look beyond the city boundaries to the broader Los Angeles economic landscape and coordinate city efforts with the growth of the more dynamic suburban areas where small manufacturing, minority entrepreneurship and service-sector employment is increasing. The greater Los Angeles area—which includes Gloria Molina's 1st Supervisorial District—is rich with redevelopment projects that attract private capital and should not be ignored in employment strategies that target underemployed and unemployed youth. Partnerships with other cities in stimulating regional growth and employment should be part of the strategy for the urban core. According to a new study by Rudy Torres and Victor Valle on the changing economic landscape of Los Angeles, "there is a new political and economic space for communities historically disconnected from the urban core. . . . Cities must articulate their economic agendas at the local and international level."

Neither Woo nor Riordan has tackled this issue, and it is incumbent that they do not myopically focus their economic policies within the city. We can no longer afford to pander to special interests that do not enhance the economic viability of the city and the region.

Los Angeles Times, April 22, 1993

Decent Wages for Economic Growth
Government must help minority businesses, which tend to be in retail and service rather than manufacturing.

MAYOR RICHARD RIORDAN knows what it takes to keep small business in Los Angeles; witness his recent success in persuading a Venice ceramics firm not to leave the city. But stopping the exit of business must go beyond such personal appeals to a long-term economic strategy. This is a formidable task, since between 1991 and 1993, Los Angeles County lost more than one hundred thousand jobs and the L.A. unemployment rate hovers at 10 percent. Strategizing for quality job growth is rarely tackled by Republicans, who view government as the nemesis of private business, creating bureaucratic mazes that prevent entrepreneurs from risking capital. Also, it's easier to attack the bureaucracy than to develop collaborative strategies to enhance the mutual interests of businesses and workers. Yet without moving forward on this latter point, any job growth will not result in stabilizing the community. Los Angeles must have job growth accompanied by a steady increase in real wages so that everyone benefits from the mayor's business plan.

Riordan does have the leadership skills that will allow him to move beyond partisan politics to create jobs. Indeed, much of Riordan's success comes from his ability to take ideas from both parties and mold a consensus that disarms critics because of its balanced view. This strength could easily allow him to develop a game plan for job growth that goes beyond streamlining government, a mantra that may win elections but provides little hope for most Angelenos, who depend on wage income.

One way to stimulate quality job growth is to use the tax system to reward entrepreneurs who provide those jobs. Riordan could work with the governor to support such a plan. A good model would be the one proposed by Kathleen Brown's campaign: the job tax credit for business. This innovative program would provide companies with tax incentives for each new job that pays $17,600 to $60,000 a year; it would reward businesses that commit to quality jobs for Californians. Another Brown proposal that bears consideration is her "California First" recommendation, which provides established California companies with a competitive edge over other bidders for public projects.

Riordan also must develop quality jobs in the inner city. The future economic stability of the city is linked to stimulating small business to stay rather than move to the suburbs. Here Riordan must focus on further developing opportunities for both existing and new minority entrepreneurs. Much of the growth within the minority-business sector is in retail and services, reflecting the national trend. A profile of Latino businesses from the recent census indicates that more than half of these are in retail and service sectors. Latino businesses in Los Angeles County provide about a half a billion dollars in annual payroll.

Unfortunately, many of the tax strategies that have been developed do not benefit the majority of Latino entrepreneurs, as the emphasis has been to provide tax breaks for manufacturing rather than service and retail. This needs to change. Here again, Brown has proposed providing direct tax relief to minority entrepreneurs, something that Riordan should consider. Brown's California Start-Up Business Tax Moratorium allows a new business to pay no taxes on income generated during its first year, with a gradual four-year phase-in to complete tax liability. This policy rewards entrepreneurs for the high risk they take during their first years and moves in the right direction in not targeting manufacturing.

Riordan understands small-business needs, but now he must address the needs of those workers who have suffered the brunt of California's recession. He must also develop a focused plan for minority entrepreneurs, as they will be key to the revitalization of the

Los Angeles economy. In an era when it is politically popular to degrade immigrants and ignore the working poor, Riordan must select strategies that benefit all Angelenos. The city's economic growth will be rooted not in corporate America, but in small businesses and workers.

Los Angeles Times, October 5, 1994

Beyond Los Angeles: Latino Politics in the Twenty-First Century

Several of my articles in the *Los Angeles Times* focused on the local politics of the region. Obviously, as Los Angeles is a largely Latino city, it was an interesting subject for political analysis. It was here that one could examine the inter-ethnic feuds that turned into political debates within the city, and also witness the legacy of racism that permeates southern California.

California is quickly becoming a largely minority state with 48 percent of its population Latino, Asian, and black, of which over 30 percent is Latino. However, two thirds of this Latino population resides in the five southern counties of Los Angeles, San Diego, Orange, Riverside, and San Bernardino.[1] Given this uneven concentration of the state's Latino population, Latino politics and participation in California is dominated by the magnitude of the Latino population of the southern region. Simply put, of the twenty-four Latino state legislative representatives, seventeen (approximately 71 percent) are from southern California. Moreover, California's most influential Latino leaders all have their roots in Los Angeles County or other surrounding southern counties and all are Democrats. These leaders include Lt. Governor Cruz Bustamante; former state Speaker of the House and Latino frontrunner for Mayor of Los Angeles Antonio Villaraigosa; L.A. County Board Supervisor Gloria Molina; Congressman Xavier Becerra; Congresswoman Lucille Roybal-Allard; State Senator Richard Polanco; and Congresswoman Loretta Sanchez.

Southern California has cultivated much of the state's Latino political leadership over the last few decades, yet the political presence of Latinos has often been a contentious process requiring extensive court battles to ensure fair representation. For example, L.A. Supervisor Gloria Molina's 1991 election and very seat on the board came about only after a lawsuit was filed by the Mexican American Legal Defense and Education Fund (MALDEF) in 1990 to develop a single-member district to allow for Latino representation on the board of supervisors. The more recent battles involving Congresswoman Loretta Sanchez (D) and Robert K. Dornan (R) in the 1994 and 1996 congressional elections illustrates how ethnicity was used not only to polarize the electorate, but also to possibly deny the incorporation of a Latina political voice during the 1990s. Although Sanchez won her congressional bid in Orange County, her victory occurred only after she successfully challenged accusations of voter fraud by Dornan and fought against the harassment of Latino voters in her district by Dornan's Republican supporters.[2]

In this new millennium, California has gone beyond the simple struggle for increased Latino representation at the state and local levels. Given term limits and the "browning" of the state, increased Latino political representation at all levels of the government is clearly evident. What is now emerging is the vying for the leadership or representative voice for this important constituency group. This was demonstrated by the contentious struggle between Congressman Xavier Becerra (D-California) and former Speaker of the Assembly Antonio Villaraigosa (D-Los Angeles) for the Los Angeles mayoral election. Both are Democrats, both are Mexican American and both were vying for the same political base. However, there could only be one winner within the Latino base of Los Angeles and that was Villaraigosa. He captured an overwhelming majority of traditional Latino voters who are working class with strong ties to their Latino immigrant roots. Unfortunately, Villaraigosa lost the race and his opponent, City Attorney James Hahn, was elected mayor of Los Angeles. Although both are liberal Democrats, a surprising coalition of black and white conservative voters resulted in Hahn's victory, despite the fact that Villaraigosa had a four to one margin of the Latino vote and Richard Riordan's endorsement. Thus, it is clear that there is still racial divide in California, particularly in areas with a largely Latino constituency like Los Angeles.[3]

The vying for Latino political leadership within the Democratic Party is not the only visible shift in California Latino politics.

The other trend is the potential growth of Latino representation within the Republican Party, particularly those of Mexican descent. Despite President Bush's poor show of support among Mexican-origin voters, the core value structure of many Mexican Americans, as with other Hispanics, is fairly conservative, thus representing the potential for increased political appeal for Republicans among this group in the future.

Although significant gains were made by Latinos at all levels of government by the end of the century, the transition toward increased political leadership did not come without painful reminders of the ethnic and racial divisions that have been so much a part of the social fabric of this region. In light of the political gains of California's Latino elected officials and the rapid rise of political participation by Latinos in the wake of Proposition 187, the Latino vote has increased in significance for both political parties. During the 2000 presidential election, the Latino vote and its electoral significance became the subject of several pre-election polls. For example, a Knight-Ridder poll, which surveyed twenty-seven hundred Hispanic voters, highlighted the social values of this population.[4] They were described as largely conservative, in that they reflect political platforms that support family values, toughness on crime and conservative views on abortion. Thus, the prospect of the Republican Party gaining entree into the Latino voter population based on its conservative values structure is clearly possible. Moreover, because four out of five of the Hispanics interviewed for the poll indicated they had never experienced discrimination, the issue of racism and ethnic identity will not, in the long run, serve as a primary binding force regarding political views. As Mexican and other Latino immigrant groups achieve economic success through subsequent generations, the significance of public programs may become less important in deciding party affiliation.

Latino immigrants may reflect the common electorate preferences over time; that is, during periods of economic prosperity, the ability to relate to a candidate in terms of core values, including cultural values, may be more significant in their decision to support a candidate without respect to party affiliation. Hence, there will be no party loyalty within the Latino population in years to come because of its diversity and the eventual economic assimilation of Latinos into mainstream America.

The Knight-Ridder poll also demonstrated that most Hispanics parallel the American political mainstream with respect to issues, values and political ideology. Although nearly three out of five Hispanics stated they were Democrats, more than one-third consider themselves to be politically conservative, while less than one-third consider themselves moderate, and even fewer to be liberal. Cuban Americans, however, are overwhelmingly Republican.

Top political concerns among Hispanic voters include education, crime and drugs, and health care—the same concerns of mainstream America. Race and ethnic affairs, immigration, and foreign affairs ranked among the lowest priorities for most Hispanic voters.

However, within the Mexican-American voting block, issues such as immigration and foreign affairs have resurfaced as important issues with the election of Mexico's President Vicente Fox. Fox, a former Coca-Cola executive, has captured the imagination and hearts of many Mexican nationals and Mexican Americans residing in the United States with his aggressive outreach efforts. In addition, President Bush has also reached out to the Mexican-origin community with his diplomatic strategies toward Mexico, despite the fact that he received a lower percentage of the Mexican-origin and Hispanic vote than did Vice President Gore during the 2000 presidential election. This was illustrated when President Bush chose Mexico as his first official diplomatic foreign visit on February 16, 2001. This action provided an important signal to the American public, especially Mexican Americans, of the centrality of U.S.-Mexico foreign policy.

The election of Presidents Fox and Bush represents a unique opportunity to build on an established relationship developed when both were governors in their respective states of Guanajuato and Texas. Both presidents share similar conservative values and business backgrounds. These presidents have also demonstrated their commitment to improving U.S.-Mexico relations and increasing binational cooperation. In addition, both have acknowledged the importance of addressing and resolving binational issues such as immigration, problems related to Mexican workers in the United States, improving border infrastructure, and enhancing NAFTA policies for small to mid-size entrepreneurs across borders.

Fox is clearly keen on cultivating the Mexican-American and Mexican immigrant support for his political agenda. This was demonstrated by his appointment of Juan Hernandez, a U.S.-born Mexican citizen, as point person on Mexican immigrant and Mexican-American issues in the United States. Fox's commitment to reaffirming the links between Mexican nationals and Mexican Americans and *la patria* (homeland) represents a rare opportunity for Mexican Americans to be included in a proactive dialogue over binational issues and concerns, including those relating to NAFTA and beyond. Moreover, Juan Hernandez's broad mission includes protecting the rights of Mexican-descent residents in the United States and re-affirming the importance of these individuals to Mexico. Many Mexican Americans identify themselves as Mexican, but until recently this affinity had not been cultivated overtly by the Mexican government.

Fox's leadership in shifting the adversarial tenor of U.S.-Mexico binational policies, combined with his recognition of the growing influence of the Mexican-American electorate, has implications for U.S. foreign policy in Mexico. As Mexican Americans and Mexican immigrants share closer cultural and ideological ties with Mexican citizens, there will be parallel political influences, as seen with Cuban Americans on U.S.-Cuba foreign policy and Jewish Americans on U.S.-Israel foreign policy. Ultimately, Fox's long-term goal is to improve Mexico's economy with the support of the Mexican-American vote on Mexican foreign and trade policy.

Notes

1. State of California, Department of Finance, *Race/Ethnic Population Estimates: Components of Change for California Counties, April 1990 to July 1998* (Sacramento: State of California, 2000).

2. Nancy Cleeland and Dexter Filkins, "Voting Dispute Deepens Rift Over Latino Group," *Los Angeles Times,* December 29, 1996, sec. A; "Furor over Election Spotlights Latino Aid-Group," *Los Angeles Times,* December 29, 1996, sec.

A; Rene Lynch and Peter M. Warren, "INS to Aid in Election Probe in O.C.," *Los Angeles Times,* December 28, 1996, sec. A.

3. "James Hahn wins L.A. mayor race," accessed at http://www.azstarnet.com/star/today/10607RLAMayor.html, June 7, 2001.

4. Steve Thomma, e-mail dated July 21, 2000, on forthcoming article on the results of the Knight-Ridder Poll in *Knight Ridder Newspapers.*

CONCLUDING
THOUGHTS

The responses to my commentaries were illustrative, and a content analysis categorized the general feelings that were expressed in them. Without a doubt, my commentaries that addressed immigration issues during the 1990s elicited the greatest response from readers. Immense hostility was expressed if a column suggested a more liberal response to state and federal policies aimed at curtailing legal or illegal immigration. The content analysis of these letters revealed the following observations:

- In all but four instances, when explicit opinions were expressed regarding Proposition 187, they were in support of the measure.
- Those who opposed 187 noted the racist and oppressive motivations of the proponents, the lack of accurate information in the framing of the debate and the majority/minority dynamics involved.
- Major areas of reader concerns included the immigrants themselves, particularly Mexican and undocumented immigrants; the perception that I was a biased observer; Proposition 187; and the role of the Mexican government in encouraging illegal immigration.

In general, the attitudes toward immigrants (149 mentions) were extremely negative and often made use of pejorative racial stereotypes. Only one letter expressed positive sentiments. In relation to this topic, feelings toward me (n = 99) were also negative in tone and made use of personal attacks on my knowledge, position in academia and ethnicity. Only two letters were laudatory and in agreement with my views on the subject of immigration. Most respondents believed my position as a Latina and columnist made me unable to objectively analyze these issues, with the additional inference that I was inherently intellectually inferior because of my ethnicity. Recurring negative themes that emerged from these letters pertained to my political views and a general contempt for me as the author of these articles and for Mexicans of my "ilk."

The negative sentiments were even more prominent toward Mexican immigrants, and the impact this group was having on American life, particularly in California. The increasing use of Spanish and influence of Catholicism, the rapid population growth relative to the nonwhite Latino population and the "criminal nature" of this group were recurring themes in these letters.

The negative attributes that were ascribed to Mexican immigrants and the Mexican government, along with the need for punitive action against both, underscore the righteous indignation of several of the respondents. Negative feelings toward the Mexican government included a general sense of the irresponsibility and corruption inherent within the political system and the politicians themselves. Moreover, there was a sense that great wealth in Mexico was being kept from citizens by the rich and those in government, and that the Mexican government encourages its citizens to migrate illegally to the United States as a way of lessening its responsibility for these people. Since many respondents believed illegal immigration was a criminal offense, explicitly comparing it to bank robbery and burglary, several letters questioned my loyalty to the United States, as well as my intelligence and my citizenship. Some respondents even encouraged me to "go back to" Mexico.

In twenty-eight letters, the word "illegal" appeared fifty-four times, an average of 1.93 times per letter, again illustrating the negative visceral response to commentaries with more moderate or "pro-

Latino" points of views. This is clearly illustrated by the following comments:

> You call yourself an economist; you might as well be another pond scum alien civil liberties union member—a defender of purulent and left wing interest. Prop 187 will prevail in the long run and illegals will be deprived of "handouts." The fact that the bulk of these recipients used fraudulent documents and happen to be of your ancestry in obtaining illegal benefits is conveniently ignored which is typical of your kind . . . Only in your dreams will your ilk make a strong voting difference despite the fact that your kind breed like hell![1]

On the other hand, this respondent provides a glimpse of the reality from a Latino perspective:

> [W]hat really inspired me to write you this letter was prompted by your well-written column . . . You touched on my exact sentiments of where many of our young troubled raza are headed today, and the need to develop concrete action in remedying that destructive plight. Your insightful column was like a breath of fresh air to "me"; it enlightens the masses which in itself is a beginning, the breaking ground towards the construction of "positive solutions" versus the defeated concept of lock-em up and throw the key away. Your article further restored my hope that there are still people out there who care enough about what's transpiring in our barrios with many of the raza.
> —Hector Gallegos

Two voices, two responses, two sides of the same coin, each reflecting their perception of my view of California's race issues in the 1990s. The first voice, a member of the majority electorate, mirrors the visceral responses of many members of the state's voting population. An electorate that is weary of the growing Latino presence in their state, and fears the impact of its diminishing control. The other voice is of a Chicano inmate who served time in the maximum security housing unit at California's Pelican Bay State Prison and whose bittersweet memories of a lost youth provide his backdrop for understanding the growing racial divide. In the view of this imprisoned Chicano: "No matter how I try to rashionalize [*sic*] or mitigate the circumstance and plight of these many youngsters in prison, they are all, to some degree, victims of a social cultural, racially divided nation . . . soldiers of misfortune."

By communicating only within our respective groups, we lose the opportunity to build new bridges across the increasing chasm between us. Failure to mark and traverse this growing distance will create even more problems during the twenty-first century. By 2020 the city of Los Angeles will be 60 percent Latino. Many of the public policy issues that are at the forefront in California now are clear proof of the impact this population is having in redefining our cultural and national identity, despite the limited participation of Latinos in the electoral process. In the short run, the threat of sustained Latino demographic growth may very well continue to create an environment where reactive exclusionary state policies define the political landscape. For example, policies such as the anti–bilingual education "Unz Initiative" and California's "Save our State Initiative" that denied services to undocumented aliens, came forth without the voice of the emerging Latino leadership. Similar policies will continue to emerge from the white conservative electorate as long as Latinos are not perceived as critical swing voters by party strategists. Significant Latino participation in national and statewide elections, combined with an effective strategy to increase the number of Latino-elected officials who can cross over ethnic lines, will be needed to put an end to divisive race-based politics.

Many of the problems that emerged in California in the 1990s were symptomatic of our own national shift in values regarding poor, disenfranchised and minority communities. During the 1990s, national bipartisan public policy was shifting away from social policies aimed at integrating excluded groups into the mainstream of society to policies where individual characteristics became the major determinants in political and economic success. But in California, these policies were darkly tinted with racial overtones—a result of the visible rapid growth of the Latino population. The reactive policies of the 1990s created a general perception among Latinos that the majority of the white electorate, particularly those in the state's Republican Party leadership, was unwilling to move towards a shared agenda of political and economic inclusion. Indeed, there was a real perception in many Latino circles that Governor Pete Wilson and the state's Republican Party were primarily focused on a strategy of sustained political exclusion. The competing perceptions of the white voting population and the state's emerging Latino majority created two distinct and mutually exclusive strategies for addressing the new immigrant issues of the 1990s.

Moreover, the growth and concentration of Latinos in the state's southern counties of Los Angeles, Orange, Riverside, San Bernardino and San Diego fueled the anti-Latino rage of many middle-class whites. This demographic concentration, combined with the economic recession of the early 1990s, the 1992 Los Angeles riots, the growing presence of Latinos in public schools and the shifting needs of aging white voters, allowed for the emergence of a zero-sum Latino/white dialogue. This dialogue became the dominant theme in electoral politics and further escalated the distance between these two groups.

The net result was not only a deepening mistrust, but also a failure on the part of Democrats and Republicans to capitalize on shared values that would in the long run strengthen their political support. In a very real sense, Latinos politically were ready during the late 1980s and early 1990s to cross over into a discussion concerning immigration, bilingual education and welfare reform. In California cities with large concentrations of Latinos, political and economic participation of local Latino leaders created the necessary backdrop for joint solutions to many of these emerging problems. However, the vast majority of the Latino leadership was denied a relevant role in either of the major parties. The marginal position of Latinos in agenda setting, however, is not the sole factor in their limited influence during most of the 1990s in state politics. As many Latinos focused a considerable amount of time on political participation within their racially gerrymandered districts, the possibility of building a relevant inter-ethnic dialogue was limited. Furthermore, since many elected Latino officials came from such racially segregated districts, their ethnic constituent base provided them with no real motivation to reconcile the deepening divide between the majority electorate and the growing Latino population. Given their ethnic isolation, it is not surprising to see the lack of offensive strategies developed by Latino elected officials to buffer the effect of racially targeted public policies. With few crossover Latino elected officials in California's legislative body, their ability to mediate the emerging conflicts was extremely limited.

Reconciling our differences early in the twenty-first century will require more than a shared dialogue. Given the rapid growth and regional concentration of Latinos, this group is ready to cross over and to make a difference both in the political and market arenas. However, what is most needed is the infrastructure to rapidly accelerate the educational process of our emerging political and business leaders. Furthermore, there is a need to recognize the widening gap between our emerging middle class and our "soldiers of misfortune." This latter group will become increasingly significant if we fail to address the issue of educational reform and student performance within segregated Latino schools. Finally, as many Latino families fall within the ranks of the working poor, we need to begin to cobble together a welfare reform strategy that does not compromise the health of our children and new immigrant families.

In many respects, Latinos in California emerged in the 1990s as a group whose power was shaped less by the influence of a civil rights agenda than by the devolution of such an agenda. There were no real Latino cultural icons for this decade since Latinos as a group did not choose to emulate the strategies of the 1960s, where civil rights legends such as Martin Luther King and César Chávez emerged. Rather, reflecting back, what we saw was an emerging local and ethnic power base of Latino elected officials who did not have sufficient skills or party support to cross political and racial boundaries. But many of these same leaders have by now garnered the necessary resources and experience to shift from the margins to the center of the state's political arena. Cruz Bustamante provided an excellent example of this in his successful bid for lieutenant governor.

Latinos may very well emerge as a successful chapter within the American legend both in politics as well as in business. However, if this group continues to be, or perceives that it is, devalued, this final chapter will be marked by further divisions, divisions that mirror the hopelessness of the Chicano convict and the bitterness of the white retiree. Until these competing voices are heard and mediated, the bridge from Latino immigrant to American citizen will continue to be frail. Thus, they too must move from the margins.

Note

1. Adela de la Torre, "Proposition 187 and Its Aftermath: Will the Tidal Wave Continue?" in *Immigration and Ethnic Communities: A Focus on Latinos,* ed. Refugio Rochin (East Lansing: Julian Samora Research Institute, Michigan State University, 1996), 104.

BIBLIOGRAPHY

Acuña, Rodolfo F. *Anything But Mexican: Chicanos in Contemporary Los Angeles.* London and New York: Verso, 1996.

Balderrama, Francisco E. *Mexican Repatriation in the 1930s.* Albuquerque: University of New Mexico Press, 1995.

Becerra, Xavier. "Single-Payer Health Reform." *Los Angeles Times,* August 26, 1994, home edition, metro, sec. B, p. 6.

Bird, Menlinda. "Rationalizing HHS Decision-Making." *Public Welfare* 53 (winter 1995): 26–34.

Black, Susan. "Bilingual Education: Melting Pot or Salad Bowl?" *Education Digest* 60 (March 1995): 53–57.

California, State of, Department of Finance. *Race/Ethnic Population Estimates: Components of Change for California Counties, April 1990 to July 1998.* Sacramento: State of California, 2000.

"The Chronicle 1999–2000 Almanac." *Chronicle of Higher Education.* Accessed at http://chronicle.com/weekly/almanac/1999/facts/6folks.htm. July 6, 2000.

Cleeland, Nancy, and Dexter Filkins. "Furor Over Election Spotlights Latino Aid-Group." *Los Angeles Times,* December 29, 1996, sec. A.

————. "Voting Dispute Deepens Rift Over Latino Group." *Los Angeles Times,* December 29, 1996, sec. A.

Cline, Zulmara, and Juan Necochea. "2000 Biliteracy." *Thrust for Educational Leadership* 24 (January 1995): 36–40.

Colino, Stacey. "The Fallout from Proposition 187." *Human Rights: Journal of the Section of Individual Rights and Responsibilities* 22 (winter 1995): 16–18.

Conforti, Joseph M., and Gisela M. Conforti. "Diversity in Sociology and Social Policy Analysis: Education Reform and the Immigration Act of 1990." *American Sociologist* 25 (summer 1994): 73–84.

de la Torre, Adela. "Proposition 187 and Its Aftermath: Will the Tidal Wave Continue?" In *Immigration and Ethnic Communities: A Focus on Latinos,* ed. Refugio Rochin. East Lansing: Julian Samora Research Institute, Michigan State University, 1996.

DeSipio, Louis. *Counting on the Latino Vote: Latinos as a New Electorate.* Charlottesville and London: University of Virginia Press, 1996.

De Snyder, V. Nelly Salgad, and Maria de Jesus Diaz-Perez. "Dios y el norte: The Perceptions of Wives of Documented and Undocumented Mexican Immigrants to the United States." *Latino Journal of Behavioral Sciences* 18 (August 1996): 283–297.

Donato, Ruben, and Carmen de Onis. "Better Middle-Schooling for Mexican Americans." *Education Digest* 61 (November 1995): 53–57.

Early, Gerald. "Ethnic Studies and American Higher Education." *Academic Questions* 7 (winter 1993/94): 48–54.

Fernandez, Christina D. "Unmasking Hopwood: How a Texas Reverse Discrimination Case Threatens Affirmative Action and College Admissions." *Hispanic Magazine* (November 1996): 57–62.

Fix, Michael E., and Jeffrey S. Passel. "Setting the Record Straight: What Are the Costs to the Public?" *Public Welfare* 52 (spring 1994): 6–17.

Garcia, Juan R. *Operation Wetback: The Mass Deportation of Mexican Undocumented Workers in 1954.* Westport, Conn.: Greenwood Press, 1980.

Gonzalez, Gilbert G. *Chicano Education in the Era of Segregation.* Philadelphia: Balch Institute Press, 1990.

"Governing Council Applauds Clinton, but Sticks by Single-Payer." *Nation's Health* 23 (December 1993): 6–8.

Greenblatt, Alan. "History of Immigration Policy." *Congressional Quarterly Weekly Report* 53 (April 1995): 1067.

Guadalupe, Patricia. "Texas Executes Another Latino Prisoner, 'Ethnic Crime Propensity' Issue Remains." *Hispanic Link Weekly Report* 18 (July 3, 2000): 1.

Gutiérrez, David. *Walls and Mirrors: Mexican Americans, Mexican Immigrants, and the Politics of Ethnicity.* Berkeley and Los Angeles: University of California Press, 1995.

Hanson, Gary R., and Lawrence Burt. *Responding to Hopwood: Using Policy Analysis Research to Re-design Scholarship Criteria.* Austin: University of Texas at Austin. Accessed at www.utexas.edu/student/research/reports/reports.html. August 7, 2000.

Hartwick, Jeffrey A. "Immigration Initiative." *Los Angeles Times,* July 22, 1994, home edition, metro, sec. B, p. 6.

Hoffman, Abraham. *Unwanted Mexican Americans in the Great Depression: Repatriation Pressures, 1929–1939.* Tucson: University of Arizona Press, 1974.

"James Hahn wins L.A. mayor race." Accessed at http://www.azstarnet.com/star/today/10607RLAMayor.html. June 7, 2001.

"Judge bars Michigan law school admissions on race." Accessed at http://www.cnn.com/2001/LAW/03/27/michigan.law.school.02/. April 29, 2001.

Kauffman, Albert. "The Hopwood Case—What It Says, What It Doesn't Say, the Future of the Case and 'the Rest of the Story'." *IRDA Newsletter.* Accessed at http://www.idra.org/Newslttr/1996/Aug/Albert.htm. April 27, 2001.

Lynch, Rene, and Peter M. Warren. "INS to Aid in Election Probe in O.C." *Los Angeles Times,* December 28, 1996, sec. A.

Martínez, Gebe. "Democrats, GOP Court Hispanic Voters." *The Detroit News* (March 5, 2000). Accessed at http://detnews.com/2000/politics/0003/06/a13–9889.htm. July 12, 2000.

Martínez, Oscar J. *Border People: Life and Society in the U.S.-Mexico Borderlands.* Tucson: University of Arizona Press, 1994.

Medina, Marcello, Jr., and Kathy Escamilla. "Language Acquisition and Gender for Limited-Language-Proficient Mexican Americans in a Maintenance Bilingual Program." *Latino Journal of Behavioral Sciences* 16 (November 1994): 422–436.

Medina, Marcello, Jr., and Shitala P. Mishra. "Relationships among Spanish Reading Achievement and Selected Content Areas for Fluent- and Limited-Spanish-Proficient Mexican Americans." *Bilingual Review* 19 (May–August 1994): 134–141.

Melendez, Melinda. "Proposition 187, Consequences for Administrators." *Thrust for Educational Leadership* 24 (January 1995): 6–10.

Office of Juvenile Justice and Delinquency Programs (OJJDP), "Violence by Juveniles, 1973–1997." Accessed at http://ojjdp.ncjrs.org/ojstatbb/qa135.html. July 25, 2000.

Perotti, Rosanna. "Employer Sanctions and the Limits of Negotiation." *Annals of the American Academy of Politics & Social Science* 534 (July 1994): 31–44.

Pipho, Chris. "Taxes, School Boards, and Higher Education." *Phi Delta Kappan* 75 (January 1994): 358–360.

Rauber, Chris. "Survey: Providers Existing Insurance." *Modern Healthcare* 28 (June 1998): 65–71.

Rochin, Refugio, ed., *Immigration and Ethnic Communities: A Focus on Latinos.* East Lansing: Julian Samora Research Institute, Michigan State University, 1996.

Rodríguez, Gregory. "The Browning of California." *New Republic* 215 (September 1996): 18–20.

Rodríguez, Norma. "Predicting the Academic Success of Mexican American and White College Students." *Latino Journal of Behavioral Sciences* 18 (August 1996): 329–343.

San Miguel, Guadalupe. *"Let All of Them Take Heed": Mexican Americans and the Campaign for Educational Equality in Texas, 1910–1981.* Austin: University of Texas Press, 1987.

Shinkman, Ron. 1997. "Latino Kids Underinsured." *Modern Healthcare* 27 (March 1997): 36.

Thilmany, Dawn D. "FLC Usage among California Growers under IRCA: An Empirical Analysis of Farm Labor Market Risk Management." *American Journal of Agricultural Economics* 78 (November 1996): 946–961.

Trevino, Robert P., and Fernando M. Trevino. "Health Care Access among Mexican Americans with Different Health Insurance." *Journal of Health Care for the Poor and Underserved* 7 (May 1996): 112–122.

University of Michigan Documents Center. *University of Michigan Affirmative Action Lawsuit.* Accessed at http://www.lib.umich.edu/libhome/ Documents.center/umaffirm.html. April 29, 2001.

Wood, Thomas E. "Group Preference Put to the Vote." *Academic Questions* 9 (fall 1996): 10–15.

INDEX

taxation, 115; employer, 27–28; health care and, 83–84, 85–86
teachers, 11, 39
tenure: and minorities, 53, 54
Texas, 9, 35, 64, 70, 78, 103
Thompson, Steve, 81
Torres, Esteban, 12, 109

undocumented workers, 4–5; and economy, 6–7; educating, 26–28; smuggling of, 20–21; social services and, 8–9
unionization, 20
United Farm Workers, 8
U.S.-Mexico border, 13–14
U.S. Supreme Court; affirmative action and, 60, 69–70; discrimination cases and, 66–67
United Way, 104
universities, 51; diversity at, 62–64; faculty at, 68–69; minority recruitment at, 70–71; reforming, 41–42
University of Arizona, 47, 70–71
University of California (UC) system, 40, 41, 43, 44, 52–53, 73
University of California, Berkeley, 59–60
University of California, Santa Barbara, 48
University of Texas, Austin, 70, 73
University of Texas law school, 64
university regents, 41–42
university trustees, 41–42
Unz, Ron, 35
Unz Initiative, 34, 35. *See also* Proposition 227

Valdez, Robert, 78
Villaraigosa, Antonio, 116, 117
Voting Rights Act, 15

wages, 65–66
Walters, Dave, 28, 31, 62

welfare reform, 4, 16, 96–97, 103–4; and health care, 80–82
welfare system: and children, 94–95
Wilson, Pete, 4, 11, 16, 21, 43, 101, 127
women, 79, 88; and businesses, 66–67; in higher education, 60–61, 65, 68–69
Woo, Michael, 112, 113
Wood, Kimba, 6

youth, 101. *See also* juveniles

ABOUT THE AUTHOR

Adela de la Torre, an agricultural economist, is the director of the Mexican American Studies and Research Center and the Hispanic Center of Excellence in the College of Medicine at the University of Arizona, where she is also a professor in the College of Public Health. She received her Ph.D. in Agricultural and Resource Economics in 1982 from the University of California, Berkeley. From 1986 to 1988, she was a Pew Postdoctoral fellow at the University of California San Francisco Institute for Health Policy Studies.

Prior to coming to the University of Arizona in 1996, Dr. de la Torre was an executive fellow in the Office of the Chancellor of the California State University system, and chaired the Chicano and Latino Studies Department at Long Beach from 1991 to 1995. Her publications and research primarily focus on health-care access and finance issues affecting the Latino community. For several years she wrote a syndicated column for the *Los Angeles Times*. Her commentaries addressed economic, political, educational, health-care and immigration issues facing Latinos in California and the nation.

She is the coauthor of *Mexican Americans and Health: ¡Sana! ¡Sana!* (2001) from the University of Arizona Press and is the editor of the forthcoming University of Arizona Press series on Mexican American Studies. She also co-edited *Building With Our Hands: New Directions in Chicana Scholarship*, published by the University of California Press in 1993.